Beyond the Boxes and Lines:
Are You Ready for the Next Step?

Copyright © Susannah Robinson and
Partnership for Talent LLC (2024)

Published by:

AUTHORSonMISSION

Acknowledgments

I am deeply grateful to the many people who have made this book possible.....

To my husband, Craig- When I suggested quitting my secure 9 to 5 job and starting my own consulting company, you didn't hesitate to instantly provide your complete support and constant encouragement. You put up with all of the early morning and late night meetings, and weekends constantly interrupted with "just one more deck" that needs to be finished. Thank you for being my first and forever partner. I couldn't have asked for a better one than you. I love you- today, tomorrow, and always.

To my daughter, Caitlin- As I always tell you, you are my "why." I love what I do for a living, but you truly give my life purpose. It has been a privilege to watch you grow into the amazing young woman you are today. Thank you for being my Disney partner and always my biggest cheerleader. I love you so, so much.

To Debra Parsons- I appreciate your day-to-day support more than you know. It is because of you that we were able to gather all of my random thoughts and experiences and put them into this book. Thank you for choosing to bring your skills to the Partnership for Talent team.

To Wally Coyle- You were an HR consultant long before it was fashionable. When I decided to start my own consultancy, you were exceedingly generous with your time, advice, and counsel. I can honestly say that Partnership for Talent would not be where it is today without your support, and I thank you.

To our Partnership for Talent clients, past, present, and (hopefully) future. Thank you for your partnership. I appreciate your trust and allowing me the opportunity to support your teams and help grow your businesses.

Table of Contents

Introduction

In the wake of the COVID-19 pandemic, the world was thrown into a state of uncertainty and chaos. People feared the unknown and the possibility of contracting the rampant virus, leading to a complete standstill in our daily routines. In addition to most businesses transitioning to a remote model, colleges and universities across the globe were forced to make the difficult decision of transitioning to virtual learning.

In addition to many years as a senior HR executive, I am privileged to teach the next generation of HR professionals at Northeastern University. As an educator, I faced a daunting challenge: how to deliver a high-quality education to my students in this new, entirely virtual landscape. Grappling with the best approach to ensure my students' learning and growth, I boldly and audaciously decided to teach my organizational design course without relying on a traditional textbook after much deliberation and careful consideration.

I recognize that others might consider my approach unorthodox. Still, I saw it as an extraordinary chance to cultivate a profound sense of engagement and foster a deeper understanding among my eager and enthusiastic students. By eschewing the conventional reliance on a textbook and embracing a more interactive and immersive learning experience, I aimed to create an educational environment that would ignite their intellectual curiosity and encourage them to think outside the box. With this innovative teaching approach, my students would acquire knowledge, develop critical thinking skills, and apply theoretical concepts to real-world scenarios.

Without a textbook, I relied solely on my lectures, casework, and class engagement. And you know what? It was a huge success, and the results of my approach were outstanding! Students were excited by the challenge of exploring complex concepts without the crutch of a textbook. They had to rely on their critical thinking skills and personal experiences to navigate the material. Witnessing their progress and growth while tackling the subject was extraordinary!

I received remarkable feedback from my students. To my pleasant surprise, they were so enamored with my teaching that they didn't miss their textbooks! They even wanted my lecture notes to become their constant companions, carrying them everywhere like their trusty sidekicks. It was as if my lecture notes became an academic Gatorade and were quenching their thirst for knowledge.

As a seasoned HR professional with extensive experience in organizational design geared toward improving business outcomes and financial results, I am pleased to introduce *Next Steps*. It offers invaluable insights and practical tools for leaders and HR professionals seeking to transform their organizations and achieve business success. This book is a must-read for professionals seeking to elevate their expertise and drive exceptional business outcomes.

With my unique and comprehensive perspective on organizational design, this book goes beyond the traditional approach. It offers practical insights that transcend conventional wisdom, providing readers with a deep understanding of how to drive positive change and achieve their mission. Within these pages, I share numerous strategies organizations can implement to foster employee engagement and create a thriving work environment. By embracing these tactics, organizations will be well-equipped to navigate the challenges of today's dynamic business landscape and unlock their full potential.

This book surpasses the basics or theoretical concepts and offers actionable steps that individuals can apply in real-world situations. Its captivating case studies, practical examples, and proven methodologies make it an invaluable resource for leaders and HR professionals aiming to transform their organizations and achieve business success.

So, if you're ready to transform your organization, improve your business results, advance your mission, and truly engage your employees, this book is for you.

It's time to take the Next Step toward organizational success!

CHAPTER 1

What is Organizational Design?

Gone are the days when organizations could rely on a rigid hierarchy and standard operating procedures to achieve their goals. Today's business landscape is dynamic and demands a strategic approach to organizational design. And it's not just about the structure; it's about creating an environment that nurtures innovation, fosters collaboration, and enables agility. In this book, we'll explore how organizational design has evolved beyond a blueprint of boxes and lines to a strategic framework that drives success and prepares organizations for the challenges of tomorrow.

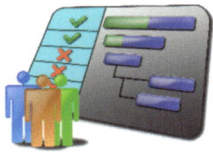

Understanding organizational design is crucial for business leaders and HR professionals in today's fast-paced business world. It's the key to unlocking an organization's full potential and driving it towards success.

Renowned author and noted expert in organizational behavior and organizational design, Richard Daft introduces a fresh perspective in his book Organizational Theory and Design.

According to Daft, organizational design isn't just a collection of facts; it's a mindset that enables us to strategically structure our organizations and mobilize resources to achieve a common goal.

The Society of Human Resource Management (SHRM) further emphasizes the importance of organizational design in accomplishing business objectives. It's not just about the structure; it's also about identifying and harnessing core competencies to drive success. Enter McKinsey Consulting, an industry leader in organizational transformation. They redefine organizational design as an integration of structure, processes, and people, all supporting strategy implementation. It's more than just rearranging boxes and lines on a chart; it's about aligning every aspect of your organization for optimal performance and results.

Organizational Design is Everywhere!

Imagine a scenario. Think back to a memorable experience at a restaurant, amusement park, hotel, hospital, or any entertainment venue. Did you ever stop to think about how organizational design influenced that experience? Whether it was the clarity of responsibilities, the seamless workflow, or the smooth handoffs, organizational design shaped your experience, even if you didn't realize it.

Lakeside resort vacation

Let's transport ourselves to a serene lakeside resort on a beautiful, warm summer day, where you spend quality time with your family. The sun is shining through the leaves of the tall trees surrounding a lake, creating a natural canopy of shade. The crisp blue water is dotted with water lilies, and the water is so clear you can see the rocks on the bottom and small fish darting in and out of their homes.

From your vantage point, the lake's shoreline is visible and dotted with colorful Adirondack chairs. A BBQ grill fills the air with the wonderful aroma of grilled vegetables and pulled pork, and a cozy hammock attached to two trees has three kids laughing as they swing back and forth. The temperature is perfect—not too hot or cold—and a pleasant breeze blows in from the lake.

As you take in the scenery with your senses, you notice the resort staff is efficiently bustling. Housekeepers quietly restock towels and linens, while maintenance workers diligently keep the grounds tidy, and bartenders deftly mix cocktails for the guests. The entire staff is in perfect harmony, with everyone smoothly executing their roles to ensure each guest has a seamless and enjoyable experience.

It's easy to take all of this for granted, but upon reflection, you realize how much organizational design impacts your experience. The resort's management has thoughtfully designed a workflow considering the staff's strengths and weaknesses and the guests' needs and desires. The result is an incredible guest experience that's always smooth and enjoyable.

From the first moment you arrived, you were greeted by friendly and helpful resort staff who seamlessly checked you in and offered suggestions about the best activities and local entertainment. You were pleasantly surprised by the level of attention to detail throughout your stay, from the beautifully appointed guest rooms to the well-maintained facilities and amenities to having your private deck to grill food and roast s'mores over the hand-built fire pit.

At every turn, the organizational design was evident in how the staff worked together, communicated effectively, and focused on providing excellent service. Whether lounging on a beach chair by the lake, enjoying a cocktail at the bar, or taking a dip in the pool, you always felt valued and appreciated. The seamless hand-offs between staff members ensured that you were never left waiting or wondering what would happen next.

Overall, this memorable experience at the lakeside resort was shaped by the management and staff's thoughtful and effective organizational design. It's a testament to the power of excellent organizational design and the impact that it can have on creating memorable and enjoyable experiences for guests. It is imperative that we recognize the power of organizational design—it is everywhere, from the restaurants you dine at to your favorite coffee shop to your town's grocery store.

In this book, we explore the practical application of organizational design, how it impacts day-to-day operations, and how strategic implementation can transform businesses. From operational structure to job design to employee practices, we uncover how organizational design can revolutionize your organization. Get ready to learn how to effectively wield this tool and watch your organization thrive in today's dynamic world!

Unlocking the magic of organizational design: A Disney World perspective

Imagine a world where employees know precisely what they're supposed to do and how their role contributes to the bigger picture. Picture a place where everyone embodies the organization's values and culture and a clear strategy guides their interactions. This idyllic world exists at Disney World.

From the moment you step foot in this magical kingdom, you'll witness firsthand how job design, workflow, and support systems magically combine to create unforgettable guest experiences. Join me on a journey through the enchanting realm of Disney World, where organizational design is taken to new heights.

Walt Disney's famous operational theory, "Do what you do so well that they will want to see it again and bring their friends," echoes throughout the park. This commitment to excellence lies at the heart of Disney World's success. And when you dig deeper, you'll uncover the many intricate components of organizational design that make it all possible.

So, whether you're a startup CEO, an up-and-coming business leader, an HR geek like me, or simply intrigued by the inner workings of a world-renowned organization, prepare to be captivated by Disney World's organizational design secrets.

Discover the transformative power of a well-crafted strategy, a highly motivated and empowered workforce, and an unwavering dedication to delivering exceptional customer experiences. Dive deep into the enchanting world of Disney World and unlock the secrets that will ignite the magic within your work environment. Prepare for a journey of inspiration, innovation, and the tools to create extraordinary moments that leave a lasting impact. Get ready to embark on a quest to unleash the true magic within your organization.

The Disney magic

Embark on an enchanting journey and delve into Disney's captivating and magical world, where dreams come true, beloved characters come to life, and extraordinary adventures await at every turn. Immerse yourself in timeless tales, heartwarming music, and unforgettable moments that will leave you with cherished memories to last a lifetime. Unveiling the secrets of organizational design, we explore the intricacies of the clarity of job design at

Disney World, unearthing valuable insights that highlight the significance of focus and specialization in creating magical experiences for visitors of all ages.

Every role at Disney World is carefully crafted to serve a specific purpose. Take, for example, the person who serves pretzels. These perfectly salted snacks are carefully crafted in the shape of Mickey Mouse and served with warm, gooey, gooey cheese sauce. These warm golden-brown delights are served by staff dedicated to ensuring they provide consistently delicious and appealing pretzels to guests. Their laser focus ensures that they understand their responsibilities and what it takes to succeed in their role. By eliminating distractions, such as sweeping or ticket-taking, they can devote their full attention to the immediate needs of the guests in front of them.

This targeted approach results in a uniquely satisfying experience for guests. It allows the cast members to prioritize the wants and needs of the customer, delivering exceptional service in the moment. Whether it's a craving for a pretzel or a craving for a mouth-watering Dole Whip and all of the delicious flavors it offers, the specialized Disney cast member meets the specific desires of each guest. No other tasks or obligations interfere with their ability to provide top-notch service.

In addition to their high level of focus and dedication, Disney cast members are also trained in the art of storytelling. They are masters at creating extraordinary moments for guests through personalized interaction with a character or genuine conversation. This attention to detail and commitment to memorable experiences set Disney apart from other theme parks.

But it's about more than just delivering excellent service and creating magical moments. Disney cast members also embody the brand's values and mission. The company's ambassadors represent its core principles of innovation, storytelling, and customer service. They understand that their role is not just a job but an opportunity to make a difference in someone's day, transport them to a magical place, and create lasting memories.

Disney World demonstrates the importance of clear communication and collaboration among its cast members. Each individual has a specific role and knows exactly what is expected of them, but they also understand how their role fits into the larger picture and where to get support when needed. This creates a sense of unity and teamwork among the cast members, allowing them to work together seamlessly and efficiently.

In addition, Disney World recognizes the value of ongoing training and development for its cast members. Employees constantly learn new skills and improve performance through regular workshops, seminars, and on-the-job coaching. This investment in their workforce ensures that guests receive top-quality service, helps retain employees, and fosters a positive work culture.

Disney World's approach to job design showcases the importance of considering individual tasks and the bigger picture when designing roles. Disney has created a winning formula for success by prioritizing specialization and collaboration. Take a page from Disney's book and find ways to blend task-focused roles with opportunities for teamwork and growth within your organization. This balance will not only benefit your employees but also contribute to the overall success of your business.

So, next time you visit Disney World, take a moment to appreciate the intricate job design that makes the magic possible. From the cast members who greet you at the entrance to those who bring beloved characters to life, each person plays a vital role in creating the unforgettable experience that is classically Disney. And by implementing similar strategies in your workplace, you, too, can create a magical and thriving organization for employees and customers.

Design Versus Structure

When most people think of organizational design, they often envision a rigid structure resembling a maze of employees and hierarchical lines on a grid. It can feel like navigating through a complex video game level while facing a boss that keeps leveling up, with power-ups hidden in the HR department. But fear not; with the right strategy and a sprinkle of humor, we can find our way to success and make work feel less like a game of hide-and-seek!

Organizational design is not solely concerned with the physical structure of a department or organization. It encompasses the seamless flow and optimal functionality of work within that structure. A well-designed organization considers not only each employee's specific roles and responsibilities but also the intricate dynamics of how those roles interact, harmoniously working together towards a unified objective. By nurturing a collaborative environment, organizations can unlock the full potential of their workforce, fostering engagement, innovation, and productivity and ultimately achieving unparalleled success.

Disney World is a prime example of this concept in action. The theme park operates on a complex system of departments, each with its unique purpose and responsibilities. With over 74,000 employees working at Disney World, it's essential to have a clear and organized design to ensure everything runs smoothly. However, its focus on creating seamless department interactions sets Disney apart from other organizations.

For instance, the custodial staff works hand-in-hand with ride operators to rinse and clean the rides, ensuring guests a safe and enjoyable experience. The culinary team collaborates with event planners to provide delicious meals at private events. This interconnectedness not only improves efficiency but also fosters a sense of teamwork and collaboration among employees.

Disney World's organizational design also allows for vertical communication between different levels of management. With multiple layers of leadership, from front-line supervisors to executives, information can effectively flow up and down within the organization. This hierarchy also creates clear lines of responsibility, so employees know who to turn to for support, guidance, or approval on various tasks.

In addition to its structured organization, Disney is known for its strong brand voice. Every aspect of the theme park embodies the "Disney magic," from the attractions to the cast members' interactions with guests. This consistent brand voice is maintained through extensive training and a robust company culture. Disney also utilizes technology to enhance the guest experience. From their Genie+ system to mobile restaurant ordering, Disney is constantly innovating and finding ways to make the park experience more convenient for guests, which not only improves customer satisfaction but also streamlines operations for employees.

Although organizational design is much more profound and intricate than meets the eye, structure is one crucial component of a broader design involving complex decision-making.

Questions arise regarding structure:

- Is it centralized or decentralized?
- Local or global?
- Functional or divisional?
- Matrix or direct?

A great example of a well-thought-out organizational design is "The Golden Arches." In fact, their design is so great that you already knew I was talking about McDonald's when you read Golden Arches. McDonald's is known for its fast and convenient service, offering a wide variety of affordable menu items such as their famous Big Mac, Chicken McNuggets, and McFlurry desserts.

Moreover, McDonald's continuously innovates its menu to cater to evolving consumer preferences and tailors its offerings to align with cuisine preferences worldwide. Through its ongoing commitment to quality, convenience, and affordability, McDonald's has established itself as a global leader in the fast-food industry. One key but less considered reason is its commitment to its organizational design.

The McDonald's difference

The choices we make in designing an organization have far-reaching implications. Let's take a closer look at McDonald's. McDonald's may have started as a humble burger joint. Still, its efficient and well-oiled organizational design has transformed it into a global fast-food empire that never fails to satisfy our cravings for tasty treats.

McDonald's operates in over 100 countries and serves millions of customers daily, making it one of the largest fast-food chains in the world. Despite its global reach, McDonald's has maintained a centralized design since its inception.

At the top of McDonald's organizational hierarchy are the CEO and his executive team, who make all significant decisions for the company. Below them are regional managers who oversee operations in different geographical regions. Under the regional managers are district managers who oversee several restaurants within a specific area.

There is a clear chain of command at the restaurant level, with the restaurant manager at the top, followed by shift managers and team leaders. Each employee knows who they report to, their responsibilities within their respective roles, and from whom they receive support. This uniformity of design allows for clear communication and efficient decision-making throughout all levels of the organization.

One benefit of this organizational design is the consistency in operations across all McDonald's locations. Whether you're enjoying a Big Mac in New York or California, you can be confident that the taste and quality will be the same. Every restaurant follows standardized procedures and uses the same ingredients, ensuring that customers receive the same mouthwatering experience no matter where they are. This dependability has significantly contributed to McDonald's success as a global brand.

Additionally, a centralized design allows for quick decision-making. With clear lines of authority and responsibility, decisions can be made quickly without going through multiple management layers. However, this type of organizational design can also have its drawbacks. The strict hierarchy can lead to top-level executives' micromanagement, limiting lower-level creativity and innovation. It can also create a disconnect between upper management and front-line employees.

While the static nature of the organizational design is beneficial in some cases, in others, it can sometimes impede growth, especially in startups. As an organization grows and evolves, it becomes crucial to actively assess and adapt the design to fit the changing needs of the business. To maintain a cohesive and efficient design, it's critical to establish clear roles and responsibilities within the organization to ensure everyone knows their role and expectations, reducing confusion and potential conflicts. Additionally, having well-defined roles allows for accountability and can promote a sense of ownership among employees. Organizational leaders must consider how and when to make these clarifications in organizational design.

> Organizational design is like a river, constantly flowing and adapting to changes. It adapts as the needs of the organization change. Its purpose is to integrate people and systems, making conscious choices that lead to improved outcomes. These out-comes encompass fulfilling a mission, achieving objectives, goals, and strategies, delivering financial results, and ultimate-ly realizing a vision.

The organizational structure is one tangible representation of the meticulous work invested in organizational design. It is a product of deliberate decision-making aimed at driving success. By defining roles, responsibilities, and relationships within the design, an organization can operate efficiently and effectively to achieve its goals.

However, conflicts are inevitable even with careful planning and intention in organizational design. For example, individuals may have different interpretations of their roles or feel that their responsibilities overlap with those of their colleagues in the workplace. This can lead to a lack of clarity, inefficiency, and even tension among employees, creating a challenging environment where productivity and teamwork must improve. Additionally, conflicting priorities and competing goals can further exacerbate these issues, making it crucial for organizations to address and manage conflicts effectively to maintain a harmonious and productive work environment.

Organizations can mitigate these potential conflicts with a strong brand voice, well-articulated company values, and clear communication channels. A well-established brand voice sets the tone for how employees should interact with each other and approach their work. It also serves as a reminder of the organization's values and mission, promoting alignment among team members. When conflicts arise, a strong brand voice can help guide the resolution process and ensure all parties work towards the same goal.

Collaboration, communication, and alignment should be emphasized when describing how a brand voice can foster positive organizational relationships. By promoting a collaboration and open communication culture, employees are encouraged to work together towards common goals, improving efficiency and creating camaraderie and teamwork among team members.

Organizational structure is a critical and probably the most well-known output of organizational design work. It defines the roles and responsibilities within an organization, clarifying who does what and how they contribute to achieving its goals. A strong brand voice and clear values can create a foundation for the structure by clearly communicating expectations and fostering a sense of accountability among team members.

Moreover, a consistent brand voice can create a sense of alignment throughout the organization. Every department, team, and individual works towards the same mission and vision. This unity helps to avoid silos and promotes cross-functional collaboration, leading to better problem-solving abilities and overall organizational success.

A robust organizational design has external benefits in addition to fostering positive relationships. It can attract like-minded individuals who align with the company's values and culture, resulting in a more cohesive and motivated workforce. By creating a consistent brand experience across all touchpoints, it can also enhance the company's reputation and increase customer loyalty.

Disney is an excellent example of a company that has established a robust organizational design that has helped weather many storms. However, other companies must realize that achieving such a level of organization is challenging and requires time, effort, and resources. Therefore, while aspiring to create a robust organizational design, companies should set achievable goals and recognize the time and hard work required to achieve excellence in this area.

It is essential to understand that companies cannot instantly replicate Disney's organizational design with simply careful planning. Instead, companies must take incremental steps toward building their organizational design that can adapt to changing circumstances, including developing an efficient decision-making process, fostering a culture of transparency and accountability, creating a clear vision and mission statement, establishing effective communication channels, adopting new technologies, and developing a reliable chain of command. By doing so, companies can create a sustainable and robust organizational design that enables them to withstand the test of time and thrive in today's competitive environment.

Outcomes of Organizational Design

Organizational design is like the sauce on a Big Mac; it is an organization's "secret sauce" determining how resources are strategically deployed within a company. It's like a roadmap, guiding where money is invested, how information flows, and what outcomes and processes should look like. But it's not just about structure—it also plays a crucial role in defining what exceptional performance means for employees. Understanding the organization's goals, strategies, and design is vital to unlocking exceptional performance and fostering meaningful interactions between team members.

A well-crafted organizational design doesn't just lead to operational efficiency and improved effectiveness; it fuels employee engagement and creates a fulfilling work experience. In today's world, it's vital to distinguish between employee satisfaction and engagement. While satisfaction refers to an employee's level of contentment with their job, engagement goes beyond that—it measures the emotional and intellectual investment an employee has in the organization. Engaged employees are passionate about their work, committed to the company's success, and willing to go above and beyond to achieve goals. A solid and well-understood organizational design can only foster this kind of dedication.

So, how exactly does organizational design impact employee engagement? Let's take a closer look at some key factors:

- *Clear Roles and Responsibilities*: A well-designed organization clearly defines roles and responsibilities for each team member. This clarity eliminates confusion and overlapping tasks, creating a sense of purpose for employees. When everyone knows what is expected of them, they can focus on their strengths and best contribute to the organization's success.

- *Effective Communication Channels*: Communication is crucial to employee engagement. A well-designed organization establishes efficient communication channels, ensuring information is shared effectively and timely, preventing misunderstandings, and fostering workplace transparency and trust.

- *Opportunities for Growth and Development:* An excellent organizational design allows employees to learn and grow within their roles, including training programs, career development plans, or even job rotations. Employees who continuously learn and improve are more likely to engage with their work actively.

- *Supportive Leadership:* An organization's leaders significantly impact employee engagement. A well-designed organization ensures that leaders have clear expectations and responsibilities, allowing them to effectively support and guide their teams.

- *Encourages Collaboration*: A robust organizational design promotes collaboration among team members. By creating cross-functional teams, clarifying hand-offs, or breaking down silos between departments, employees can work together towards common goals and share knowledge and resources.

- *Emphasize Company Values*: A well-designed organization should align with the company's values and culture. Incorporating these values into the design makes employees more likely to feel connected to the organization's mission and purpose, leading to higher engagement and job satisfaction, approaching work the "right" way, and fulfilling the company's mission.

We've all seen companies with content employees who need more engagement. Strong employee engagement is a game-changer—it drives business outcomes, propels missions forward, and even boosts company valuations. It's an ongoing journey that hinges on answering three critical questions for employees:

> Where do I fit?
> How can I contribute?
> Where can I go?

Effective organizational design is like a well-choreographed dance routine. It answers crucial questions and creates a positive experience, keeping employees engaged and moving in tandem for the long haul.

However, the benefits of good organizational design extend beyond employee engagement. It also impacts customer service, satisfaction, and business results. Referring back to the legendary example of Disney, a well-designed organization that delivers customer satisfaction aligning seamlessly with its objectives and, in turn, driving exceptional guest experiences = an organization poised to have extraordinary success.

David Ulrich, a pioneer in organizational design, emphasizes its immense impact on business outcomes. Ulrich went as far as to say, *"Organizational design has four times the impact on a business outcome than individual competencies."*[1] Executing skillfully can transform a company's ability to achieve its goals, whether financial growth, superior performance, or mission advancement.

Conversely, poorly executed organizational design exposes significant roles, responsibilities, communication, and accountability gaps. It erodes capacity, capability, and ultimately the bottom line, affecting cash flow, customer delivery, employee engagement, and retention. Good organizational design

---

[1] Schawbel, D. (2017, April 5). *Dave Ulrich: Organization Has 4 Time The Impact On Business Results As Individual.* Forbes.
https://www.forbes.com/sites/danschawbel/2017/04/05/dave-ulrich-organization-has-4x-the-impact-on-business-results-as-individual/?sh=761e7752517e

emerges as a powerful catalyst for positive results, while a misaligned one can have detrimental consequences.

In short, organizational design's impact goes far beyond the surface. It's a critical tool for optimizing performance, driving engagement, and ultimately shaping an organization's success. So, whether you're an organizational leader, HR practitioner, or aspiring business professional, recognizing its importance is the first step towards unlocking its transformative potential.

Influences on Organizational Design

Discovering the best organizational design for a company is a challenging feat. Numerous factors come into play, both from the outside world and within the company.

> One of the key drivers of organizational design decisions is the level of complexity within the company. How complex is the organization? How challenging must it be to cater to custom-ers' needs? These questions influence crucial aspects such as the company's structure, job design, and employee practices.

Understanding the level of complexity of a company's business and markets can provide valuable insights into the company's needed structure, job designs, and employee practices. A complex organization typically has multiple layers of management, a diverse workforce, a wide range of products or services, and operates in numerous markets. Catering to the needs of such a diverse customer base can be challenging and requires a highly responsive and adaptable team.

Such organizations also require flexible and agile structures that adapt to changing market conditions. Job designs need to be efficient and effective while crafting employee practices to support innovation and creativity specifically. Understanding the complexity level is crucial in developing an efficient, adaptable, customer-focused organization that can thrive in a rapidly changing business landscape.

Its dynamic nature is another important consideration when analyzing a business to ensure appropriate design choices. The speed at which a company needs to adapt and change in response to market trends and shifts is crucial in determining the design components needed to stay ahead of the competition. Startups, for instance, are characterized by their agility and flexibility in responding to rapidly changing market conditions or technology needs. In contrast, more extensive, mature businesses may find it more challenging to adapt quickly to new changes because their organizations are more rigid and less responsive. It is also essential to consider where a business is in its lifecycle regarding its size.

Small businesses have different requirements than large corporations, and the organizational or business lifecycle stage can significantly impact how a business adapts and evolves. For instance, a small company in hyper-growth mode may require a different approach to organizational design than a mature business focused on maintaining market share. Therefore, to understand a business fully, it is crucial to consider its dynamic nature and stage in the organizational or business lifecycle. Doing so can provide more comprehensive and nuanced insights into how a business operates and strategizes for the future.

Furthermore, the level of bureaucratic control required can significantly impact how organizations operate, particularly those that serve government entities. These organizations must adhere to countless checklists and processes to comply with the governing body's regulations and protocols. These can range from strict documentation requirements to rigorous reporting structures, significantly impacting how the organization functions. In some cases, this level of bureaucracy can create inefficiencies, leading to slower decision-making processes and endless red tape. However, in other cases, it can also provide the accountability necessary to ensure that public services are delivered effectively and efficiently. Ultimately, the level of bureaucratic control required will depend on the nature of the organization and

its mandate, with government entities typically requiring the most stringent adherence to bureaucratic procedures.

Last but not least, let's remember the stakeholders. The Board of Directors, employees, customers, and government entities all influence the needs that the company's organizational design must meet.

The Board of Directors, as the highest level of management in a corporation, is responsible for protecting shareholders, making decisions, and setting strategic goals. They often have a more long-term vision and ensure the organization's success.

Employees are also crucial stakeholders on the front lines of the organization's daily operations. Their input is valuable in identifying areas for improvement and implementing changes to increase efficiency and productivity, as they are the ones in the trenches who often see how it is.

Customers, or clients, are another critical stakeholder group, as their satisfaction with the organization directly impacts its success. A customer-centric approach to organizational design can increase loyalty, retention, and positive word-of-mouth recommendations.

Considering the impact on all stakeholders helps shape an organization's organizational design. Richard Daft explains in his renowned organizational design textbook that organizations are like "open systems."[2] They take inputs such as people, information, and financial resources and transform them into outputs in the form of products and services. The organizational design influences this transformation, determining the quality and nature of the outputs.

Organizational design is a complex and intricate, yet fascinating (remember, I said I was a nerd) discipline that balances external and internal factors to create the most appropriate blueprint for an individual company's short and long-term success. The external factors include market trends, competition, and regulations, while internal factors include company culture, mission, and values. An effective organizational design aligns the company's overall design

---

[2] Daft, R. L., & Armstrong, A. (2009). *Organization Theory and Design*. Nelson Education.

with its goals and objectives, creating an environment that promotes creativity, innovation, and productivity.

One of organizational design's main challenges is balancing the company's long-term goals with its short-term needs. This balancing act often requires organizations to be as limber as a Cirque Du Soleil performer and deeply understand the company's current capabilities and potential for growth and expansion. It also requires a thorough analysis of the company's industry and market to identify the most promising opportunities for that growth.

More adroitly put, organizational design is the art of balancing complexity and goals by deciphering external and internal factors. It is critical to a company's success and requires careful consideration and planning to create an effective design that promotes growth, innovation, and productivity. By aligning the company's goals with its culture, mission, values, and goals, an effective organizational design can create a work environment that inspires and motivates employees to achieve their full potential and drive the company toward success.

Intentional and Ongoing Organizational Design

In the ever-changing business world, two types of organizational design work hold the key to success: intentional and ongoing. Intentional design results from deliberate decision-making, incorporating feedback, and a constant willingness to seek improvement. It acknowledges that perfection is a myth and that every choice has consequences. That's why being intentional with your organizational design is paramount.

> But here's the catch: organizational design is never static. Or-ganizations are living, breathing creations. Organizational de-sign is an ongoing process that needs to adapt and evolve along with the ever-shifting landscape of technology, custom-er demands, and industry competition. Just think about the rise of Amazon, starting as a humble online bookstore and now dominating the global market.

The rise of Amazon is a clear example of how intentional organizational design can impact a company's success. What began as a humble online bookstore in 1995 has become a dominant global market leader, expanding into numerous industries such as cloud computing, artificial intelligence, and e-commerce. Amazon's success can be attributed to its unique business model, which focuses on highly efficient logistics, customer obsession, innovation, and operational excellence. Its founder and leadership team's intentionality to continue molding its organizational design to capitalize on market opportunities.

The company's organizational design has been critical to its success, with a hierarchical structure fostering clear communication and decision-making lines. Amazon's innovative culture encourages experimentation and risk-taking, leading to the development of innovative products such as the Kindle e-reader, Amazon Prime, and Alexa. The company has also successfully leveraged data and analytics to drive better business decisions, from recommendation algorithms to supply chain optimization. Overall, Amazon's success is a testament to the power of intentional and ongoing organizational design, which can help companies succeed and dominate the market.

Or Apple, which is constantly reinventing its product line to stay ahead. Over time, Apple's ability to adapt and improve its products, both transformationally and incrementally, has been instrumental in establishing itself as a significant player in the tech industry. While the Apple II may be a thing of the past, Apple didn't let that stop them from pushing forward and creating new products that can meet the ever-changing needs of consumers.

Apple has consistently shaken up industries with its innovative releases, from the iPhone to the iPad. By prioritizing design, functionality, and user experience, Apple has solidified its position as a leader in technological innovation, setting trends that are now commonplace in the market. Other companies looking to achieve sustainable growth and stay competitive can learn something from Apple's approach to product development. In Apple's case, its entrepreneurial organizational design is critical to its success.

As leaders, we must stay informed about internal happenings and be mindful of external factors that can significantly impact our design decisions. By adopting an intentional and ongoing organizational design mindset, we can proactively make minor, incremental adjustments rather than resorting to drastic overhauls. This approach allows us to stay agile and adaptable, ensuring our organizations are well-prepared to navigate our ever-changing business landscape.

> Organizational design is a complex and ever-evolving process; remember, when you change one area of your design, it's essential to recognize that it will inevitably impact many others.

By embracing intentional and ongoing organizational design practices, you'll unlock the potential for sustained success in this ever-evolving world of business and innovation. Taking a holistic approach to design and considering the interconnectedness of various elements and interdependencies between different parts of the organization will enable you to create harmonious and practical solutions that stand the test of time.

Minor, incremental tweaks become a valuable tool in continuously improving organizational design. These minor changes can streamline processes, improve communication channels, and enhance employee engagement. Organizations that adopt an ongoing design mentality can stay adaptable, agile, and responsive to changing trends in their industry.

The advantage of incremental design changes over wholesale transformations is that they require less dislocation and adjustment periods for employees, which results in a smooth and less distracting transition. When an organization significantly overhauls its design, it can cause unrest and uncertainty among employees. As a result, employees can become less productive at work, resist change, or even depart the organization altogether. However, there are times when a wholesale transformation is necessary, such as in organizational restructuring or mergers and acquisitions. During these times of transformational change, organizations should take extra care to communicate with employees and involve them in the change process. Careful planning and robust implementation support can mitigate the potential negative impacts of wholesale changes in organizational design. Ultimately, organizations need to be flexible and responsive, continually evaluating and adjusting their design to ensure that they remain competitive and able to deliver the value that their stakeholders expect.

Adopting a proactive and continuous approach to organizational change is vital in today's dynamic business landscape. Just as working out builds muscle and often leads to soreness, building "muscle memory" in organizational design empowers companies to navigate any transformation confidently. Similar to how soreness indicates progress in physical fitness, the challenges faced while building organizational design signify growth and development. By embracing these challenges, companies strengthen their ability to adapt and thrive amidst change, ultimately achieving long-term success.

Why is integrating change and change management into the daily fabric of your organization important? By doing so, you eliminate the fear associated with change, make it a natural and seamless part of your operations, and help to create an environment where success becomes more attainable and less daunting as your team becomes accustomed to embracing and adapting to new challenges and opportunities. No longer will you have to endure traumatizing upheavals; instead, you'll foster a culture of agility and resilience that propels your organization toward sustained growth and achievement. By outwardly embracing change, you can create an environment where your employees actively bring you ideas for changes that will move the business forward.

Whether it's a shift in staffing, strategy, markets, economics, or the external and internal environment, every change is an opportunity to learn and improve. After each transformational moment, take a pause and evaluate.

- Can we approach this differently?

- Can we do it better? If so, how? If we can't, why is this the ceiling for effectiveness?

- Is the structure working?

- Are our job designs effective?

- Do our employee practices align with our goals?

Equipped with these valuable insights, you can confidently make the necessary adjustments to adapt better, thrive, and excel in the ever-evolving landscape. Embrace the transformative power of ongoing organizational change, continuously refining strategies and processes to position your organization for sustained long-term success. By embracing a proactive approach and staying agile, your organization will be well-prepared to navigate challenges and seize opportunities that arise along the way.

The Next Step

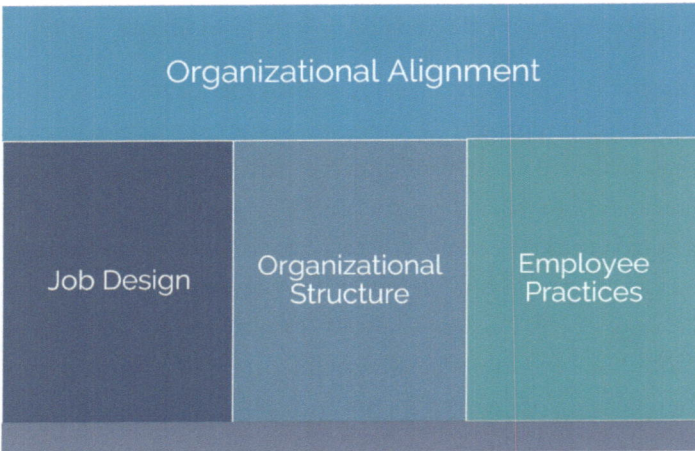

I am thrilled to introduce "The Next Step"—an innovative model I have developed to walk through organizational design and ensure alignment with business goals and objectives. In today's fast-paced and competitive business landscape, having a clear direction and ensuring all team members work towards common goals is crucial. "The Next Step" provides a structured look at aligning teams, streamlining decision-making, and maximizing efficiency. With this model, we can unlock the full potential of our organization and take the next step toward success. I aim to help you align your organizational design with your operational goals through a step-by-step process.

In our exploration, we will delve into four fundamental components of design: organizational alignment, job design, organizational structure, and employee practices. These components are crucial to understanding how they interact and influence one another and increasing our chances of creating a winning organizational design. By comprehending the intricate dynamics between these elements, we can pave the way for achieving our objectives with greater precision and effectiveness.

One question guides our approach at every step: "Are we aligned?" We'll delve into what alignment means for each aspect of organizational design. Our ultimate goal is to align job design, organizational structure, and employee practices with our strategy, values, mission, and operational goals.

> To assess our organizational design, we must first understand our organization's identity and purpose.
>
> • Who are we?
> • What values do we hold?
> • What are our capabilities?

Various factors intricately shape our design decisions and ultimate success. By deeply understanding our organization's identity and purpose, we can align our design choices with our values, capabilities, and overarching goals. This alignment guarantees that our organizational structure, processes, and resources are finely tuned for optimal success. These factors serve as guiding principles, influencing and molding our design decisions and ultimately playing a pivotal role in our organization's triumph.

Just as a skilled captain assesses the strengths and weaknesses of their crew before setting sail, understanding our strengths and weaknesses is vital for effectively analyzing our organization. By gaining this self-awareness, we can chart a clear course toward success in reaching our goals.

Organizational Understanding

As we discuss this topic, please reflect on the organizations you're currently involved with or have been part of. These comparisons will help us apply organizational design principles and the "Next Step" model. The "Next Step" model is not merely an abstract concept; it is the practical work that organizations, business leaders, and HR professionals undertake daily.

We must understand who we are and what we aim to achieve to succeed. Every business or organization has its own set of goals and objectives, which drive its operations and decision-making. By aligning our strategies with these goals, we can create objectives and ultimately meet our goals.

Organizational design, the art of structuring and aligning various components within a business or organization, is immensely significant in shaping and influencing outcomes. By meticulously crafting the framework and optimizing its elements, leaders can catalyze positive impact and drive organizational success to new heights.

Let's embark on a journey to explore this subject further, uncovering its intricacies and discovering the transformative potential it holds for achieving unparalleled excellence.

CHAPTER 2

Ensuring Organizational Alignment

Organizational Understanding and Alignment

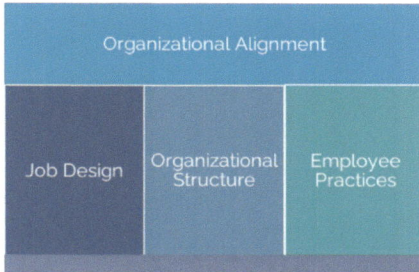

Creating a successful business requires thoughtful consideration of organizational design. Establishing alignment among all design aspects is crucial to ensure they work together harmoniously. This alignment is influenced by various elements such as culture, purpose, strategy, values, and goals. You can propel your organization toward its intended outcomes by carefully designing an organization that supports and nurtures these components. This strategic approach fosters cohesion, collaboration, and long-term success.

A practical example of thoughtful organizational design leading to the success of a real-world business is Google. Google's organization is designed to foster innovation, collaboration, and agility. They have a flat structure that promotes open communication and quick decision-making, broad jobs that encourage overlap and teamwork, and cutting-edge employee practices and offerings that encourage employees to focus on meeting key milestones and propelling the company forward. Their culture encourages creativity and risk-taking, allowing employees to explore new ideas and drive continuous improvement. By aligning their organizational design with their purpose of organizing the world's information, Google has become a global leader in technology and internet-related services.

What is Organizational Alignment?

Clarity is the key to success in a purposeful organization. It's about making sure your employees understand their roles, their impact, and how they contribute to the bigger picture. This understanding motivates your team to give their best every day. They know where they fit, how they make a difference, and what opportunities lie ahead for them.

> As leaders, it's our job to provide these answers:
>
> - *Where do I fit?* Help employees find their place in the organization and understand how their role links to the mission.
> - *How can I contribute?* Show employees how their efforts contribute to the organization's success, giving them a sense of purpose and fulfillment.
> - *Where can I go?* Provide a clear path for growth and development, empowering employees to reach their full potential.

We must align our organizational design with our organizational purpose to achieve this. By leading with our mission, vision, and core values, we can define our unique culture and set clear expectations for employee engagement.

We also need to identify key engagement points and align on the professional characteristics that matter most to us. This will allow us to develop organizational capabilities and leadership competencies and implement consistent talent management processes.

Let's unlock the power of purpose and create a workplace where employees thrive and organizations succeed.

Talent Vision

Talent vision is the compass that guides managers, candidates, and employees toward the organization we aspire to become. It's not just a one-size-fits-all concept—it's intensely personal to each organization, tailor-made to align with the business strategy and fuel success. This vision empowers employees, offering them a clear roadmap to develop, grow, and ultimately thrive within the organization.

As the former CHRO of a group of YMCAs, I witnessed the transformative power of talent vision firsthand. A memorable conversation with one of my HR Generalists stands out. They shared how the talent vision served as a guiding light, a justification for the tasks assigned. The insight gained from this vision helped shape our HR strategic goals, offering focus and clarity to our talent management initiatives and even their day-to-day work.

But that's not all. Our talent vision goes beyond words; it captures the very essence of our organizational culture. It sets the stage for employees to experience a profound sense of purpose and fulfillment while working with us. Engagement and productivity soar when individuals align themselves with our organization and what it stands for.

So, how can you create a talent vision that genuinely resonates with your team? Start by understanding your organizational goals and values and ask yourself the following questions:

- What is your company's ultimate purpose?

- What are your core beliefs and principles?

- What is your vision for your organization in simple terms?

- How do you envision your organization's future?

- In a more down-to-earth way.....what do you want your organization to *be*?

These key elements should form the foundation for shaping and realizing your comprehensive talent vision, guiding your strategic approach, and fostering a culture of excellence within your organization.

Next, it is crucial to carefully consider and empathize with your valuable employees' diverse needs, ambitions, and aspirations. Understanding their goals and desires can foster a supportive and nurturing work environment, increasing job satisfaction and productivity.

- What motivates them?

- How can their individual strengths and skills be utilized to contribute to the organization's overall success?

- Again....simplified, what do you want your employees to *feel*?

Why settle for mediocrity when you can embrace the power of talent vision? Watch your organization thrive, see your employees excel, and make success the norm. It's like having a magic wand but without all the hocus pocus!

For one organization I have worked with in the past, the below picture beautifully encapsulated everything we aspired our organization to be, showcasing our core values, vision, and commitment to excellence. It symbolized our relentless pursuit of innovation, teamwork, and customer satisfaction, reminding us of the heights we aimed to reach and the impact we sought to make in our industry.

We want our organization to be

INCLUSIVE & ENGAGED	HIGH PERFORMING	LEARNING	INNOVATIVE & PROGRESSIVE
An inclusive and engaging organization where opportunities for meaningful work are plentiful, and staff feel recognized and valued for their contributions	A high performing organization where expectations and feedback are clear and staff feel confident in seeking support when needed	A learning organization where training and development are valued and staff are encouraged and supported to reach their full potential	An innovative organization where collaborative risk taking is encouraged, best practices are freely shared, and progressive ideas to maximize our impact are fully utilized
APPRECIATED	SUPPORTED	INSPIRED	ACCOUNTABLE

We want our employees to feel

By highlighting transparently to the team what we wanted their organization to be and how we wanted their employees to feel, we could engage everyone in driving to the same organizational vision and holding each other accountable if things began to drift off track. Here's how they described it:

- Our organization is committed to fostering an inclusive and engaged environment where high performance, continuous learning, innovation, and progress are valued. Defining what these aspirations mean to our people is crucial for their success and collective growth.

- Our employees can expect us to provide a supportive and appreciative culture. We aim to inspire them by nurturing their talents and enabling them to reach their full potential.

- Accountability is also a key component. We believe in empowering our employees to take ownership of their work and contribute to the organization's success.

- By cultivating a sense of appreciation, support, inspiration, and accountability, we strive to create an environment where our employees feel valued and motivated to excel.

Each organization's vision will be distinctive, providing the foundation for creating real employee engagement. Simply assessing employee satisfaction with benefits doesn't provide the necessary information to understand their engagement with the company. We must also understand their level of commitment, loyalty, and motivation to drive performance and innovation and contribute their passion and extra efforts to our success.

Engagement is critical to maintaining a high-performing workforce. As leaders, we want our employees to feel engaged, motivated to succeed, and empowered to take the initiative; it requires open communication channels where employees feel comfortable sharing their thoughts, ideas, and concerns. Promoting transparency, authenticity, and respect is crucial in fostering this environment.

To chart our course and truly connect, we must intimately know the organization we strive to be and the emotions we want our team to feel. This understanding becomes our compass, guiding us to ask the right questions. Through this, we gauge our progress, spot areas that need attention, and fuel our ongoing growth and development.

McKinsey & Company

You may remember McKinsey & Company's discussions of the "War for Talent" in the late 1990s. This concept was based on the premise that a company's most valuable asset is its human resources; as such, finding and retaining top talent was crucial for sustained success.

The War for Talent is characterized by fierce competition among companies to attract and retain the best employees, primarily focusing on high-potential individuals who could be groomed for leadership positions. They emphasized the importance of talent management practices such as leadership development, performance management, and succession planning.

Having a clarified talent vision can help companies stand out in this war for talent because it allows them to describe to candidates what it is like to be an employee in that organization.

Another key concept related to talent vision is the "employee value proposition," which refers to the unique benefits and opportunities an organization offers its employees in exchange for their contributions. A compelling employee value proposition should align with the company's overall strategy and culture and be communicated clearly and consistently to potential and current employees.

> In recent years, there has been a shift towards a more holistic approach to talent vision focusing on employee well-being and work-life balance. This has led to the emergence of terms such as "employee experience" and "talent mobility," priori-tizing creating a positive workplace culture and developing flexible career paths for employees.

Ultimately, a well-crafted talent vision is critical for organizational success. It enables companies to attract and retain the best talent, build a strong employer brand, and foster a culture of innovation and growth. By investing in talent management practices and staying attuned to emerging trends, organizations can position themselves for long-term success in a rapidly changing business landscape.

A-Team (not the Ed Sheeran song, but the organizational version)

One well-known concept related to talent is "A-players." A-players possess exceptional skills and characteristics that make them valuable additions to any organization. They are high performers who consistently deliver results that exceed expectations and are widely recognized as top performers within their respective fields—think Michael Jordan, Taylor Swift, Denzel Washington, or Serena Williams.

But it's not just about individual talent—it's also about creating a strong team of A-players. The concept of the "A-team" is often used in organizations with cohesive, high-performing teams that work together towards a common goal. These teams comprise individuals who complement each other's strengths and weaknesses, allowing for collaboration and innovation.

So, how can organizations attract and retain their A-team? It all starts with a strong employer brand. Your employer brand is your organization's reputation as an employer. It encompasses everything from your company culture, values, mission, and vision to your hiring process, employee benefits, and overall workplace experience.

Firms with a strong talent strategy emphasize recruiting, developing, and retaining top performers crucial for long-term growth and prosperity. In addition to acknowledging and incentivizing these high achievers, companies may establish rigorous hiring practices to attract and retain them.

> Another term related to talent vision is "talent pipeline." This concept refers to creating a continuous flow of high-potential individuals who can fill essential leadership and management positions. A strong talent pipeline is integral to the long-term success of any organization, as it ensures that the company has a reservoir of skilled and capable individuals ready to take on new challenges and responsibilities.

Organizations can also foster a culture of continuous learning and development to support the growth and retention of their teams, including providing opportunities for training, mentoring, and career advancement. By investing in their employee's professional development, organizations attract top talent and show a commitment to nurturing and retaining their employees.

Furthermore, creating an inclusive and diverse work environment is crucial for attracting and retaining high-caliber talent. According to research, diversity and inclusion positively impact organizational performance and innovation.

By promoting diversity in all aspects of the workplace, from recruitment to leadership positions, organizations can attract a wider pool of talented individuals and create a sense of belonging for all employees.

To build a robust talent pipeline, companies may invest in programs that identify and develop promising employees, provide learning and career growth opportunities, and foster a culture of continuous improvement and performance. These initiatives help organizations create a pool of talent equipped to drive the organization's goals and objectives forward over time.

To sum it up, setting talent vision is a critical aspect of organizational design, as it sets the foundation for recruiting, developing, and retaining top talent. By prioritizing talent vision, companies can position themselves for sustained success in an increasingly competitive business landscape.

Alignment to Values

Organizational design is crucial in bringing together the organization's and its employees' values. Whether it's a corporation, company, nonprofit, or educational institution, each entity develops its own set of core values. And hey, much like the rise of fanny packs as a fashion statement, core values became quite trendy in the 1990s.

We strategically introduced core values to rally and unite everyone within the organization around a shared set of characteristics deemed vital for its long-term success. These values serve as guiding principles, shaping the culture and behavior of individuals and fostering a sense of purpose, alignment, and cohesion throughout the organization. By establishing and upholding these core values, the organization can cultivate a strong and resilient foundation, enabling it to navigate challenges, make informed decisions, and achieve sustainable growth in today's dynamic and competitive business landscape.

Therefore, the key lies in forging a robust connection and collectively striving towards a shared objective!

Values are the solid bedrock upon which an organization's culture is meticulously built. They are not merely words on a page; they are the guiding principles that permeate every aspect of the organization's conduct and behavior, influencing the actions of employees, management, and other stakeholders. These values shape the very essence of the organization, dictating its reputation, recruitment efforts, and public persona. They embody the organization's commitment to integrity, innovation, inclusivity, and excellence and serve as a compass to navigate the ever-evolving business landscape.

How Apple used core values to inspire

To illustrate how values contribute to an organization's reputation, consider the case of Apple. This company prides itself on quality, innovation, and design. Apple's core values go beyond merely producing top-notch products; they also focus on positively impacting society. The organization's commitment to excellent design and quality control has earned it a reputation as a top-tier tech brand. Apple's values also translate into the company's marketing strategies, which is evident in its "Think Different" campaign, which epitomizes innovation, creativity, and nonconformity.

Apple's Think Different campaign, launched in 1997, was a groundbreaking advertising initiative that showcased the company's core values of creativity, innovation, and individuality. The campaign featured iconic figures such as Albert Einstein, Mahatma Gandhi, and Martin Luther King Jr., emphasizing their unique contributions to society and inspiring viewers to think outside the box.

This campaign promoted Apple's products and reflected the organization's belief in challenging the status quo and breaking barriers. It encapsulated Apple's commitment to creating products that were not just functional but also beautifully designed and user-friendly. Through this campaign, Apple established itself as a brand that celebrates diversity, embraces originality, and encourages individuals to think differently. Even today, this campaign is a testament to Apple's unwavering values and inspires people worldwide.

Googling its way to a stellar public persona

Furthermore, values are integral to any company's recruitment efforts. Prospective employees are increasingly keen on working for companies that align with their values and beliefs. Firms that articulate clear and compelling values are more likely to attract top talent than those that do not. For example, Google, a company with a mission to organize the world's information, promotes a culture of openness, collaborative work, and a nonhierarchical structure. Google's strong emphasis on its values has helped the company attract and retain some of the world's best technical talent. Besides, employees who share a company's values tend to be more engaged and perform better, leading to higher productivity and success. A well-defined understanding of who you are and your values allows organizations to attract individuals best suited to help move that particular organization forward.

Another way values contribute to an organization's image is through its public persona. This is especially true today, with growing interest in corporate social responsibility. Consumers, investors, and other stakeholders are concerned about organizations' impact on the environment, the community, and the wider society. Companies that uphold strong values aligned with their stakeholders' interests are perceived positively and are more likely to enjoy customer loyalty, trust, and support.

Ensuring an organization's design aligns with its values is foundational to shaping culture, behavior, and performance at all levels. Values are essential to an organization's reputation, recruitment efforts, public persona, and much more, making them critical to its success. By upholding and promoting strong values, organizations can improve their performance, strengthen their brand, and positively impact society.

Once, a CEO intriguingly described the need for company values to me. He related his 40 manufacturing sites spread across the globe as resembling the Wild West. Visualizing himself donning a hat and riding from fort to fort on his trusty horse, he aimed to ensure that as he rode from fort to fort, there was a set of common threads weaving them all together. These were their core values and a collective adherence to integrity, respect, innovation, and competitiveness. (perhaps not the right core values for everyone, but it worked for this organization!). He wanted to ensure he knew what to expect when he got there. This captivating approach offered a unique perspective and highlighted the CEO's dedication to fostering a culture that thrived upon these fundamental principles.

When an organization firmly upholds embedded values, employees can quickly spot alignment within the organizational design. However, if things feel "off" to an employee, it's often due to a misalignment between the organizational design and the organization's values. Whether employee practices or job expectations, ensuring harmony between the organizational design and its values is critical for a cohesive and thriving workplace.

Organizational design plays a crucial role in supporting the culture and values of an organization. Strongly embedded values within an organization create a shared understanding of what is essential. These values provide a framework for decision-making, problem-solving, and goal-setting. When employees understand the organization's values, they are more likely to identify with them and feel motivated to work towards achieving organizational goals. The organizational design helps provide a framework for employees to accomplish the organization's work within the construct of the values.

Non-profit organizational design

Let's take the example of a non-profit organization that values diversity and inclusivity. The organization's mission is to promote social justice and equality for all individuals, regardless of their background. The organizational design of this non-profit includes hiring practices that prioritize diversity and inclusivity. This means that the hiring committee actively seeks candidates from diverse backgrounds and provides equal opportunities for all applicants, regardless of race, gender, religion, or sexual orientation.

As a result of this robust value system aligned with the organizational design, employees within the non-profit recognize the importance of their work. They are motivated to uphold the values of diversity and inclusivity in all their activities. They understand that the organizational design intends to support these values, demonstrating to employees that their work is meaningful and supports the organization's greater mission.

On the other hand, if the job expectations or employee practices do not align with the organization's values, employees may not feel engaged or energized. For example, suppose a company that values work-life balance requires employees to work long hours or doesn't provide flexible working arrangements. In that case, it may lead to a misalignment between the organizational design and values. Employees may feel that the company's actions contradict the stated values, which can decrease job satisfaction and lead to higher turnover.

Organizational design and strongly embedded values go hand in hand. When organizational design is aligned with the company values, employees feel more motivated and committed to achieving organizational goals. Conversely, when values and the organizational design are misaligned, employees may need help understanding their role and feel disconnected from the greater mission. This is why organizations must ensure that their organizational design aligns with their values to create a strong, cohesive culture.

Alignment to Strengths and Capabilities

When well understood and defined, organizational capabilities can set a company apart. They're a unique blend of skills, processes, technologies, expertise, and good old human ingenuity that make an organization stand out. You cannot buy these capabilities off the shelf; they're cultivated within the company.

Think of them as an organization's superpowers. They give the company the strength to take on challenges, implement strategies, and drive talent requirements. These capabilities are necessary for the organization's design to succeed.

So, when making organizational design decisions, it's crucial to tap into these capabilities. They hold the key to unlocking success and achieving strategic objectives. After all, a company is only as strong as its capabilities.

Organizational capabilities are what distinguish a company from its competitors. They arise from a company's unique combination of skills, processes, technologies, expertise, and human abilities. The organization's capacity to undertake activities and deliver competitive advantage is critical to success in today's business environment.

Let's take the case of a software development company. One of their core organizational capabilities is their ability to deliver customized software solutions to their clients. This capability arises from their software architecture, programming languages, project management, and a deep understanding of their customers' needs. Their ability to assemble these knowledge areas into practical software products differentiates them from their competitors.

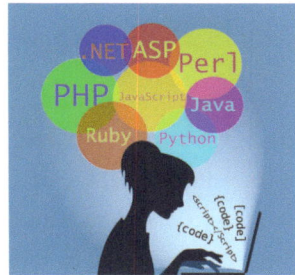

The company's capability begins with its software architecture expertise. The team profoundly understands software design patterns, integration, and deployment. They also have experience with the latest technologies and can leverage them to design scalable, highly available systems. This skill set enables them to start each project with a sound foundation.

Next, the team's programming language expertise is crucial. They are skilled in various programming languages such as Java, Python, C++, and JavaScript. This expertise enables them to build robust and scalable solutions that handle large amounts of data and complex business logic.

Additionally, the team's deployment expertise is essential. They are skilled in using modern DevOps tools and technologies such as Kubernetes, Jenkins, and Docker and have experience in automated testing, deployment, and monitoring. This skill set enables them to deliver reliable, highly available, and scalable solutions.

Finally, and perhaps most importantly, the team's in-depth understanding of their customer's businesses and the needs that their products meet helps them design packages with just the right level of technical prowess.....not too stripped down but not overly complex.

Organizational capabilities enable a company to provide unique and high-quality services. Organizations need to determine not only their capabilities but also what they need to be to be successful. For instance, in a software development company's context, these capabilities encompass diverse skills, cutting-edge technologies, deep expertise, and intense relationship building. By leveraging this powerful combination, the company can deliver exceptional products that meet and exceed customer expectations.

Furthermore, by continually building on these capabilities, companies can gain a significant competitive advantage in the marketplace. This advantage allows them to stay ahead of the curve, adapt to changing industry landscapes, and consistently expand and enhance their services to serve their clients better. This long-term approach ensures that the company remains at the forefront of innovation and maintains its position as a leader in its respective industry.

Assessing organizational capabilities is vital and indispensable in the organizational design process. It enables businesses to identify their strengths and weaknesses, ensuring the design aligns with their needs and goals. However, organizational design may sometimes need to align with an organization's current capabilities. In such cases, these capabilities either need to be built or the design and long-term goals of the organization changed to support the capabilities the organization does have. Organizations can unlock their true potential and thrive in today's dynamic business landscape by embracing a forward-thinking approach and strategies that surpass current capabilities and committing to building and developing the ones needed for success.

Organizational capability assessment

An organizational capability assessment is a critical and comprehensive process that allows companies to gain deep insights into their current capabilities and unlock their true potential. By conducting this assessment, stakeholders can accurately identify and bridge any gaps between their existing capabilities and desired objectives. This involves meticulously evaluating the capabilities required to align with the company's strategy, ensuring a strategic and well-informed approach to achieving organizational goals.

This evaluation not only enables organizations to identify areas for improvement and potential changes to organizational design, processes, talent, and job roles, but it also empowers them to gain valuable insights into their current capabilities. Companies can gather and analyze data by conducting a comprehensive capability assessment to identify gaps or deficiencies hindering their progress. This, in turn, allows them to create a strategic plan that outlines the necessary steps, processes, and improvements required to achieve their goals, ensuring a more effective and efficient path toward success.

Organizational strengths

Organizational strengths and capabilities may seem similar, but distinct concepts contribute to an organization's success. Think of organizational strength as a deep understanding of where your organization shines the brightest. It's about identifying the unique abilities, talents, and resources that set your organization apart.

Similar to how every superhero squad has powerhouses like Superman, Thor, and Hulk, every organization also has specific functions, divisions, and teams that excel and stand out. These superhero-like teams possess unique abilities and expertise, contributing to the organization's success. Just as the Avengers combine their strengths to save the world, organizations leverage the diverse talents of their teams to achieve remarkable results. Understanding and optimizing these superhero teams within an organizational context is crucial for fostering effective collaboration and innovation and ultimately driving success.

These standout areas are like your organization's superpowers, fueling its success and enabling it to excel in its industry. By recognizing and harnessing these strengths, organizations can more effectively achieve their goals and overcome challenges.

Moreover, understanding organizational strength allows leaders to make strategic decisions, allocate resources wisely, and build teams that complement each other's abilities. It also helps identify improvement and development areas, ensuring long-term growth and sustainability.

So, while organizational capability refers to an organization's overall capacity and potential, organizational strength focuses on the unique strengths and standout qualities that make it exceptional—its competency, if you will. Embracing and nurturing these strengths is vital to unlocking an organization's full potential and driving its continued success. Let's dive deeper into the secrets of organizational strength!

Have you ever wondered how to harness your unique strengths effectively and cultivate the necessary capabilities to achieve your goals? One highly effective approach is conducting an organizational SWOT analysis, as shown in the diagram below.

	Strengths	Weaknesses	
➤ What do you do well? ➤ What unique resources can you draw on? ➤ What key organizational capabilities do you have?	Strengths	Weaknesses	➤ What could you improve? ➤ Where do you have fewer resources than others? ➤ What functional gaps do you have? ➤ Where do we not currently have capabilities?
➤ What opportunities are open to you? ➤ What trends could you take advantage of? ➤ How can you turn your strengths into opportunities?	Opportunities	Threats	➤ What threats could harm you? ➤ What threats do your weaknesses expose you to?

A SWOT analysis empowers individuals and organizations to gain a comprehensive understanding of their current position and strategically plan for future success by thoroughly examining the internal strengths and weaknesses, as well as external opportunities and threats. If you're seeking a proven method to unlock your potential and navigate toward your aspirations, consider diving into the insightful realm of SWOT analysis.

Similar to formulating a new product development strategy, conducting this analysis allows us to thoroughly evaluate the strengths, weaknesses, opportunities, and threats within the context of our organization. By delving into a comprehensive SWOT analysis, we can gain valuable insights that guide us in determining the most effective direction for our efforts and identifying critical areas for further development and growth. This ensures that our organizational design thrives and aligns with the organization's goals. Let's dive in and unlock your organization's full potential.

Alignment to strategy

The success of business strategies dramatically depends on the seamless interplay between organizational design and well-defined strategic planning. Ensuring the chosen design components align perfectly with an organization's strategic goals is crucial to driving improvements and positive change. When the workforce fully comprehends the purpose and objectives of the proposed changes, and these changes are in complete harmony with the overall strategy, it creates an environment that fosters efficiency, teamwork, and collaboration.

Which comes first, strategy or structure?

A well-thought-out organizational design is pivotal in effectively supporting the organizational strategy. When contemplating the interplay between structure and strategy, it is imperative to consider the capabilities and constraints of the organizational structure. This thought-provoking question arises: Should the structure be aligned with the strategy, or should the structure shape the strategy? Striking the right balance between the two is critical to achieving organizational success and adaptability in a dynamic business environment. Let's delve into this intriguing dilemma and uncover which deserves the spotlight first.

On one hand, aligning structure with strategy entails crafting the organizational framework to meet specific strategic goals. Communicating objectives and fostering effective coordination among various departments or teams can enhance collaboration and synergy. Organizations can maximize their resources toward desired outcomes by tailoring the structure to complement the strategy.

Conversely, proponents argue that organizational structures can also influence strategies. Factors such as company hierarchy, reporting lines, and decision-making processes shape how strategies are conceived and executed. For instance, a top-down hierarchical structure may foster a conventional and risk-averse strategy, whereas a flatter, decentralized structure could stimulate innovation and experimentation.

The relationship between organizational structure and strategy is intricate and interdependent, necessitating thoughtful reflection and continual assessment to ensure alignment and effectiveness. Leaders must remain agile in adjusting structures to support evolving strategies and goals while consistently evaluating how the current structure impacts strategy implementation. This perpetual balancing act is paramount for organizations to sustain competitiveness and success in today's rapidly evolving business landscape.

Discover the power of strategy and structure in organizational success

Dr. Dean Cleavenger, an Associate Professor of Management at the University of Central Florida (UCF), lectured on precisely these questions related to organizational design and strategy. Below is this lecture, "Structure should reflect the organization's strategy and strategy should reflect its structure. Which comes first?"[3]:

> In one of my past lives, I spent a fair amount of my time teaching strategic management and I used to always make the statement "strategy follows structure," probably because I was teaching the students strategy, and I wanted them to be mindful that a successful strategy will tap into the existing organizational structure. In other words, if you have an organization that you're analyzing and building a strategy for, you need to consider how that organization is structured, if it's departmentalized by a geographic region then you have operations in one place and operations in another location may be overseas or maybe within the United States you need a strategy that recognizes that unique structure or you build a strategy around something you can't implement very well.
>
> And as I was teaching many years later I was doing some preparation for the classroom and I was thinking, oh, I want to talk to them about structure following strategy, or what was it again, strategy follows structure and I honestly couldn't remember, so I looked it up ..... and I found reasoning for both and all this time I thought of it as a one-way thing because I was teaching strategy. I thought people who are thinking about building a strategy need to look at the structure. Well, conversely, people who are looking at a building a structure need to consider the

strategy so both strategy follows structure and also structure needs to be built out facilitate the strategy of the organization and had not really thought about that it makes complete sense. Here we're talking about organizational design and structure how you organize yourself whether it's geographically or some other way....depends to a large extent on what your strategic goals are what your long-term plan is, and you should change your organizational structure over time to facilitate this execution of the strategy that you have in place.

Now both can be changed, you can change an organization's strategy for sure but you can also change an organizational structure. It takes a little bit of time and effort to do so because sometimes literally changing your organizational structure means you change where people work from you change what locations they are that can be costly and consume a lot of resources for the organization but it's a it's a investment in creating an organizational structure that can better[3] facilitate the execution of a strategy. That is key to being competitive in the marketplace, so we ought to always examine the organization's strategy when we're looking at opportunities to change the way in which we're structured.

I've always emphasized the crucial relationship between strategy and structure. And let me tell you, this connection is truly game-changing!

Picture this: If you're crafting a winning strategy for an organization, you must consider its existing structure. Understanding the unique aspects of the structure is essential for designing a perfectly aligned strategy.

But here's the kicker—it works the other way around, too! When considering a building or organizational structure, you must consider the strategy it needs to achieve. Because guess what? Both strategies and structures have a mutual dependency.

---

[3] https://www.youtube.com/watch?v=LeSMW8ryPuc&list=PLKG-KpSVo5HzANQ_Ibmrfec0CyYxM3e6_

But don't forget, the structure is not set in stone. You have the power to shape it to execute your strategic goals effectively. Of course, changing your strategy or structure is no small feat. It requires careful planning, investment, and a willingness to disrupt the status quo. But trust me, it's an investment that will pay off big time.

Here's my advice: Whether you're a seasoned strategist mapping out business goals or a meticulous structural planner designing organizational frameworks, it is crucial to continually and closely monitor the dynamic interplay between strategy and structure. Understanding the intricate relationship between these two key elements is critical for maintaining a competitive edge in today's ever-evolving marketplace. Stay vigilant and adaptable to thrive in the face of change!

When changing strategies for an organization or even a department, assessing whether the current organizational design will support the new approach is critical. More often than not, changing strategy without changing the organizational design will result in a return to the old strategy.

Alignment to Goals and Objectives

Strategy guides an organization toward its goals and objectives, which are the specific achievements we aim to achieve. While strategies provide a long-term direction, goals and objectives have a shorter timeframe.

Ensuring that organizational design aligns well with the goals and objectives set by the organization is crucial. Remember, we are discussing broad organizational design here, not just structure. Some examples:

- Jobs should be well-designed to enable the achievement of the goals and objectives.

- For recruiting, it is essential to ensure that you have the right talent pool in different divisions or functions to achieve objectives.

- Over time, the organization can nurture specific roles to grow into higher positions, such as transitioning specialist roles into management roles.

- Well-aligned compensation programs can motivate and retain top talent while reinforcing the chosen design by offering competitive salaries and benefits to employees in line with their roles and responsibilities.

- Establishing clear communication channels and decision-making processes is crucial to successful organizational design. This practice includes setting up regular team meetings and encouraging open dialogue between all levels of the organization. By fostering a culture of transparency and collaboration, teams can work together effectively towards common goals.

- Another critical aspect of effective organizational design is incorporating employee feedback at all levels. This process can include conducting employee surveys, soliciting suggestions for improvement, and being open to constructive criticism. Involving employees in the process makes them feel valued and engaged in shaping the organization, resulting in higher job satisfaction and productivity.

By aligning your organizational design correctly, you maximize the possibility of achieving your goals and objectives.

It is also crucial to review and update the organizational design as needed. As businesses evolve and grow, they may need to adjust the structure to accommodate shifting needs and priorities. Organizations can ensure their design supports their goals and objectives by staying proactive and adaptive.

Effective organizational design is essential for success in today's constantly changing business landscape. Organizations can create a structure that promotes collaboration, innovation, and growth by considering factors such as culture, communication, feedback, and adaptability. With an optimized design, teams can work together seamlessly towards shared goals, leading to long-term success for the organization.

External Factors

External factors play a pivotal role in shaping organizational design decisions. These factors encompass various dimensions, such as the ever-evolving competitive landscape, the dynamic legislative framework, the prevailing economic conditions, the ever-changing needs and preferences of customers, the reliability of suppliers, the availability of raw materials, the allocation of financial resources, and the vibrant external talent market.

Gaining a profound understanding of the external influences on a particular organization is paramount to crafting effective and efficient organizational designs. Organizations must continuously adapt their designs to external factors, ensuring a seamless alignment between their internal operations and the ever-evolving external environment.

Aligning organizational design with external factors is crucial for the success and sustainability of a company. The competitive landscape, for example, can influence an organization's design and strategy, as it determines the level of competition and the market share of different businesses. A competitive landscape saturated with strong rivals requires a different organizational design than a less competitive landscape with fewer companies vying for the same market space.

In addition to the competitive landscape, legislative and economic conditions also play a significant role in shaping organizational design. Changes in government regulations and legislation, such as new environmental regulations or restrictions on certain materials, can necessitate changes in operational structures, job design, and employee processes. Economic conditions, including fluctuations in the market and availability of financial resources, can also impact organizational design decisions.

Customers and suppliers are equally critical external factors that businesses must consider when designing their organizations. The organization's structure, job designs, and processes must meet customers' needs and demands. Suppliers also play a crucial role in organizational design, as the availability and quality of raw materials and resources can impact production processes and, in turn, the organization's design.

Finally, the availability of talent in the external talent market can significantly influence organizational design. The structure and composition of the organization's workforce must reflect the skills and expertise required by a company. The availability of talent in some geographical regions or industries can impact decisions related to organizational design, such as outsourcing or setting up satellite offices.

To summarize, aligning organizational design with external factors is essential for a business's success. External factors such as the competitive landscape, legislative and economic conditions, customers and suppliers, raw materials, financial resources, and the availability of talent in the external market must be considered to ensure the organization remains competitive, efficient, and effective in meeting business objectives.

COVID-19, a modern external factor

The recent COVID-19 pandemic exemplifies how organizations must align their design with external factors to ensure success. The pandemic disrupted global supply chains, caused economic uncertainties, sent many workers home for long, remote periods, and transformed customer preferences and behaviors. Organizations had to reassess their structures, job designs, and employee practices to remain viable and sustainable in this rapidly changing environment.

For instance, many restaurants and cafes had to modify their organizational design to align with customer preferences for online ordering, home delivery, or curbside pickup. Some had to cease their dine-in services completely, while others seamlessly integrated online ordering platforms into their business models.

Similarly, many retail companies had to shift from traditional brick-and-mortar stores to e-commerce platforms to meet the surge in online shopping. Adjusting their organizational designs through expanded delivery options, virtual consultations, and digital payment methods allowed them to thrive while meeting changing customer needs.

The COVID-19 pandemic sparked innovations and creative solutions in healthcare. Remote monitoring technologies, telehealth, and virtual consultations transformed the delivery of healthcare services, with many institutions adopting new technologies to connect patients with health professionals in real-time. These innovations required a shift in the organizational design of healthcare institutions, enabling them to deliver fast, efficient, and quality care while satisfying patients' safety and health concerns.

The COVID-19 pandemic is a prime example of how aligning organizational design with external factors is essential to remain viable and sustainable in a changing environment. Organizations that modified their structures, processes, and operations to adapt to the pandemic's realities continued providing exceptional services, meeting changing customer needs, and maintaining their competitive edge.

E-commerce and external factors

A prime example of how aligning organizational design with external factors is necessary in the modern-day business landscape is the emergence of e-commerce in the retail industry. With the Millennials, particularly Gen-Y and Gen-Z generations, becoming a larger and more significant component of the disposable income pool in the world, online shopping has skyrocketed. Companies have had to adjust their organizational design and operations to align with this external factor.

To remain competitive in e-commerce, retailers have had to rethink their product offerings, supply chain management, and customer experiences. For example, a traditional brick-and-mortar retailer's organizational design may have revolved around physical store locations and product displays. However, an e-commerce retailer needs a different organizational design focusing on digital channels, efficient fulfillment, and customer-centric operations.

To achieve this alignment, retailers have invested in technology and data analytics to optimize their supply chains, improve delivery times, and personalize the customer experience.

They have also introduced new roles, such as e-commerce managers, data analysts, and digital marketing specialists, to ensure they have the necessary expertise and skills to compete in e-commerce.

The legal and economic environment has also shaped the organizational design of e-commerce retailers. For example, recent data privacy regulations such as the GDPR (General Data Protection Regulation) and CCPA (California Consumer Privacy Act) have required online retailers to implement new processes and employee practices to ensure compliance.

These transformations require a comprehensive understanding of the changing dynamics and an agile approach to meet the challenges and opportunities of the digital era. Businesses must embrace innovative strategies and organizational designs to thrive in this ever-evolving market.

The emergence of e-commerce in the retail industry is a prime example of how external factors can significantly impact organizational design decisions. By adapting their structures, job designs, and employee practices, companies can help stay ahead of the competition and drive long-term growth and success.

Validating Alignment

Validating alignment in organizational design is a process that enables you to assess the efficacy of your organizational design relative to a series of critical aspects of success. It involves asking yourself key questions to evaluate whether the resources, structures, and strategies that make up your organizational design ensure your business is well-positioned to thrive amidst challenges that can influence its trajectory.

Validating alignment in organizational design involves several steps. The first step is to assess the external factors that affect your business, such as shifts in the market, government regulations, and changes in customer preferences. This step involves gathering data from external sources such as customer surveys, expert analysis, and industry reports to understand the changing external environment and its impact on your business.

The second step is to review your organization's internal operations and interplay to evaluate how well they align with your strategy, goals and objectives, purpose, values, and vision. This step involves examining your organizational design components, such as business processes, team structures, communication systems, and each team member's role.

After conducting the external and internal reviews, the third step involves identifying the gaps in your organizational design. These gaps could be in the form of inadequacies in talent acquisition, poor communication between teams, process inefficiencies, misaligned employee practices, or insufficient resources. Addressing these gaps is essential since they can limit your business's ability to operate effectively in a constantly changing external environment.

The final step in validating alignment in organizational design is to take corrective action to close the identified gaps in your organizational design, including streamlining processes, optimizing team structures, acquiring new talent, and investing in new technologies. These actions are all crucial for achieving organizational success. Ensuring that the corrective action aligns with the broader organizational goal and can facilitate long-term strategic success amidst increasing external pressures is critical.

Validating alignment in organizational design is essential to remain competitive in a rapidly changing external environment. Businesses can remain agile and responsive by assessing external factors and aligning internal processes and operations. It includes reviewing internal operations, identifying gaps, and taking corrective action measures. Through the process, businesses can streamline organizational structures, optimize resources and talent, and become more resilient to external influences.

Competitive advantages in organizational design

Every organization has unique strengths that give it an edge over its rivals— whether in terms of its products, customer experience, or pricing strategy. To maximize these advantages and ensure alignment with your overall strategic goals, tailor your organizational design accordingly.

So, how do you validate your organizational design in this context? For starters, it's important to ask yourself some key questions.

- Does the design fit with your overall strategy, and is it well-suited to the competitive landscape in your industry?
- Will it work equally well in each of your key markets, and does it take full advantage of your unique strengths and advantages?

To answer these questions effectively, conducting a comprehensive analysis of your organizational design and competitive landscape is essential. This process might involve looking at your organization's overall market position, examining key competitors, and identifying areas in which your organization is particularly strong or weak. Consider conducting surveys or focus groups to gather insights from key stakeholders—including staff members, customers, and industry experts.

Ultimately, the key to validating alignment in organizational design is to ensure that every aspect of your design works harmoniously toward your overall strategic goals. Creating a flexible, agile structure responsive to changing market conditions is crucial. By leveraging your unique strengths, you can outperform your rivals. With the right approach, your organizational design can become a powerful weapon in your arsenal, allowing you to achieve business results, stay ahead of the curve, and drive lasting success in your industry.

Organization design in divisions or geographies

When considering organizational design in relation to organizational relationships, it is crucial to acknowledge the interplay between divisions or geographies. Ask yourself, does the design recognize the relationship between corporate entities and geographies or divisions? If properly aligned, it will clarify where each contributes value to the whole and validate the design regarding talent within the organization. Remember, the goal is to create a design that provides opportunities for key players to add value, driving the organization forward.

Your organizational design should highlight roles contributing to and creating employee growth and development opportunities. Consider areas where your talent pool may have strengths or weaknesses. By addressing these questions, you can validate the organizational design in relation to the relationships within the business.

It is also important to know the limiting factors that may impact alignment. These constraints or potential roadblocks may make implementing the design challenging.

Additionally, company stakeholders or owners may have specific interests and expectations for the organization. Consider factors such as community engagement or a family-centric culture, especially if it's a family-owned business. Furthermore, information or system limitations may also prevent specific organizational changes from taking place.

> A friendly reminder: a design must align seamlessly with the corporate culture to be effective and successful. And hey, don't forget to give it some periodic checks as it progresses—after all, even the best-laid plans can sometimes use a little tweaking.

Are We Aligned?

The Next Step model emphasizes the significance of aligning the various components of organizational design to achieve organizational success. While conducting all assessments may not always be feasible, we should prioritize the most critical ones to ensure optimal success.

As we continuously learn, evolve, and adapt along our journey, we must ensure that our employees fully comprehend the underlying reasons behind the changes we implement. By effectively demonstrating how these changes align harmoniously with our core values, purpose, strategy, goals, and objectives, we address the ever-present question that lingers in the minds of our valued team members: "Why?" Let's delve into the realm of possibilities and explore how we can create a workplace environment that not only evolves but also ignites excitement and enthusiasm.

> - What outcomes are we trying to achieve as an organization?
> - Does our organizational design currently support these? Why or why not?
> - How will the strategic imperatives drive our organizational design thinking?
> - What about our culture or values should we keep in mind when thinking of our organizational design?

CHAPTER 3

The Hidden Power of Job Design

Job design plays a pivotal role in organizational design. Over the years, I have worked with many organizations facing business challenges or looking to continue to drive successful growth.

As I worked with these business leaders, I repeatedly heard something was "wrong" with the structure. More often than not, the root of the problem was not the structure but the job design.

Why do we emphasize job design? It ensures we proactively design our jobs to achieve the organization's objectives. By aligning the components of each role and their interconnections, we maximize organizational capabilities. We leverage our strengths and competencies to identify gaps and deliberately address them. And guess what? One way to bridge these gaps is through superior job design. When contemplating roles, it's crucial to consider the size, scope, accountabilities, and deliverables involved.

> Job design encompasses responsibility, accountability, per-formance expectations, and development paths. It also in-volves creating strong recruitment and selection processes and developing organizational matrices.

Creating a framework that aligns our jobs with our goals and brings out the best in our organization—let's do it!

Back to the happiest place on Earth

Let's take a trip down memory lane, back to the case study I mentioned at the beginning of this book. Remember Disney World? We delved into the intricacies of job sizes and scopes, ensuring that each role perfectly harmonizes with others to achieve desired outcomes. Employees must understand their specific accountabilities and contributions to the overall organizational goals. As leaders, we play a vital role in clearly articulating these expectations.

But here's the intriguing twist: well-designed jobs can be one of the most important things we can do to benefit our teams and individual employees. When roles are too narrow, it leaves individuals without enough challenges, hindering their growth and potential. On the other hand, overly broad jobs can overwhelm even the most capable individuals, akin to juggling a never-ending list of tasks that seem impossible to complete within a standard workday or by just one person. Striking the right balance between breadth and depth is vital to maximizing efficiency, fostering personal development, and ultimately finding the perfect fit for a position that brings out the best in individuals and drives organizational success.

It's fun to stay at the YMCA

When I started working at the YMCA, the Aquatics Directors had a never-ending list of responsibilities. From lifeguarding and swim instruction to program development, talent acquisition, business operations, marketing, and community engagement, they had to wear multiple hats. The problem was the compensation and experience required for these positions didn't always match up, making it challenging to find the right candidates.

We decided to make a change. We redefined the role of the Aquatics Directors, focusing on staff training and product delivery. We delegated some general management tasks to more seasoned individuals and administrative and marketing tasks to those skilled in the appropriate functional areas. This adjustment made finding suitable candidates more successful in their roles more accessible and, even better....ensured our Aquatics Directors were more engaged daily—leading to happier members who benefitted the organization's overall mission.

Having a broad range of responsibilities can quickly overwhelm individuals, causing disengagement. It also leads to confusion among employees when everyone seems to be doing everything. Defining roles and responsibilities is crucial for job satisfaction, engagement, and customer service. Without it, employees may leave, resulting in a never-ending recruiting, hiring, and onboarding cycle.

We achieved the goal of creating a stronger and more effective team by streamlining the Aquatics Directors' role and providing clear expectations. This strategic approach increased job satisfaction among team members and led to higher employee retention rates, meaning our ability to have experienced employees and smoother day-to-day operations. With a shared understanding of responsibilities and improved communication channels, our team was better equipped to deliver exceptional results and drive success in our organization.

So, precisely what is job design?

Job design is a crucial aspect of organizational management, encompassing categorizing tasks into distinct jobs based on various factors such as timing, methodology, and sequence. Moreover, job design entails identifying and aligning the skills and competencies needed to effectively carry out the assigned tasks. It also ensures that each job, when taken as a collective, contributes in a specific way to achieving business or organizational results. A meticulously crafted job design ensures that individuals responsible for performing particular tasks resonate with a workflow conducted logically and cohesively. By focusing on optimizing job design, organizations can enhance productivity, employee engagement, and overall operational efficiency.

Instilling a sense of accomplishment and satisfaction among employees fosters a strong connection and commitment to the company's goals and values, think highly engaged employees. Moreover, simplifying job explanations, establishing clear task assignments, and ensuring employees know where to go to get support when needed can enhance the overall efficiency and effectiveness of the workforce.

This approach provides a better alignment of employees with the job design, reduces the chances of random task allocation, and promotes a more systematic workflow within the organization.

Benefits of Job Design

Job design plays a vital role in boosting motivation and commitment within an organization. It fosters a seamless connection between employees and clarifies their organizational roles. By answering fundamental questions like "Where do I fit?" and "How can I contribute?", job design establishes a strong link between job duties and outcomes. Additionally, it aligns individual roles with the overarching goals of the organization. As a result, employees find their work more meaningful, knowing they are contributing to a more significant cause.

Return to Disney World

Disney World excels in aligning talent with the perfect job fit. By carefully selecting skilled individuals and designing job roles, they create an environment where employees feel motivated, engaged, and confident that they have the best job in the company. As they continue to grow and develop their skills and competencies, they progress through the organization, finding the right roles for them at each stage.

Job design is critical in enhancing organizational efficiency, fostering quality work, employee engagement, and creating memorable customer experiences. By carefully considering individuals' skills and experiences, job design also becomes integral to succession planning. With this valuable knowledge, organizations can develop and design effective succession plans that ensure a smooth transition of talent and expertise, paving the way for long-term success.

Good job design is critical to enhancing the quality of your organization's output. Revising and aligning tasks with the organization's goals can prevent disgruntlement and foster a more harmonious work environment. Proper job design can lead to clarity and reduce friction among employees, both new and existing. Imagine the frustration of newly hired individuals discovering that others already perform tasks they thought would be assigned to them when they accepted the job and not understanding who is supposed to do what; often, this happens when jobs are not designed properly or, moreover, not appropriately communicated to everyone within the organization. Such miscommunication not only strains relationships but also hampers employee motivation and engagement. It may prompt talented employees to seek opportunities elsewhere.

Furthermore, balancing the impact of job design on employee engagement is imperative. It can be the deciding factor between retaining and losing a skilled workforce. With well-defined job roles, assigning accountability for work outcomes becomes easier, reducing blame games and organizational inefficiencies.

Built Ford Tough

One real-life example of creating good job design within an organization is Ford Motor Company. In the early 20th century, Ford implemented a progressive assembly line system, leading to mass production and significant cost reductions. However, the work could have been more varied and exciting, often leading to employee dissatisfaction and high turnover rates.

To address the issue, Ford implemented job design changes that aimed to increase employee satisfaction and efficiency. Ford introduced job rotation, which involved assigning employees to tasks on the assembly line. This approach gave employees a sense of variety and excitement, ultimately boosting their motivation. Secondly, they organized work into small, manageable tasks that were easy to learn, reducing errors and improving efficiency. Lastly, Ford introduced rest breaks from specific tasks, allowing employees to focus on other tasks as an intentional component of their job to break up the monotony of work and reduce fatigue.

These job design changes significantly increased employee satisfaction and reduced turnover rates. Employees reported higher levels of engagement, motivation, and job satisfaction. The improvements in job design also increased efficiency and productivity, helping Ford further reduce costs and improve profitability.

Ford used research, observation, and experimentation to develop their job design. They used scientific management principles to analyze work processes, identify inefficiencies and redundancies, and develop more efficient and effective working methods. The company also conducted surveys and focus groups to understand employee needs and preferences, which informed their job design decisions.

Ford's success in making job design changes demonstrates the importance of creating a job design that meets the organization's and its employees' needs. By taking a systematic and data-driven approach to job design, organizations can boost engagement, motivation, and productivity and achieve their goals more efficiently and effectively.

Key Elements of Job Design

Job design entails meticulous consideration and organization of tasks that must be accomplished, including allocating or reassigning current duties and integrating new functions essential for a job or business. Job design aims to create motivation by carefully crafting and structuring a job's tasks, responsibilities, and roles. It involves considering factors such as skill variety, task significance, autonomy, and feedback to ensure employees feel purpose and fulfillment. Organizations can enhance employee motivation and increase productivity and job satisfaction through effective design.

Well-designed jobs ignite employees' desire for such positions and constantly inspire them to strive for excellence. When thoughtfully crafted, jobs align with employees' strengths and passions, fostering a sense of purpose and fulfillment. For instance, imagine a job in which a software engineer can work on cutting-edge technologies, collaborate with a diverse team, and contribute to solving complex problems. Such a role can inspire and motivate employees to go above and beyond, unleashing their full potential and driving outstanding results.

With well-defined jobs, organizations can have multiple candidates for open jobs and be able to select the best fit. I wholeheartedly advocate for creating jobs that elicit healthy competition among potential employees. This approach signifies that the jobs are meticulously defined and purposeful, ensuring meaningful work that resonates with individuals on a deeper level. Organizations can attract passionate individuals driven to significantly impact their roles by fostering an environment where job seekers actively compete for opportunities.

In one of my previous roles as CHRO, I relentlessly pursued the CEO to be selected for the role because the job design was so remarkable that it was obvious how I would contribute to the organization's results. I clearly understood my role and what the organization needed me to achieve, envisioning myself in the job even before they offered it.

Job design encompasses several principles that are crucial for effective task management. Examples of these principles include:

- *Clearly defining tasks:* A detailed description of the tasks to be completed.

- *Setting specific starting and stopping points for each task*: Establishing specific time frames or milestones for starting and completing tasks.

- *Establishing a clear line of sight for work outcomes*: Ensuring that the desired outcomes and goals of the work are communicated and understood.

- *Identifying interaction or intersection points:* Helping employees understand where their job fits in with the broader system helps make transitions and handoffs more seamless, ensuring the total system works well

While many organizations are proficient in defining the scope of a role, they frequently require assistance in effectively conveying the significance of an employee's work in contributing to the organization's overall success. Here are a few practical steps toward improving communication:

- Clearly articulate the organization's goals and objectives, emphasizing how each employee's contributions play a vital role in achieving them.
- Foster open and transparent communication channels, encouraging employees to share their ideas, concerns, and suggestions.
- Provide regular feedback and recognition to acknowledge and appreciate the impact of individual efforts on the organization's success.
- Implement effective communication tools and platforms to facilitate seamless information sharing and collaboration across teams.
- Encourage cross-departmental interactions and knowledge-sharing sessions to enhance understanding of how different roles and responsibilities align towards common goals.
- Conduct regular meetings or workshops to discuss the organization's progress and ensure that employees understand how their work directly contributes to that progress.
- Offer training and development opportunities to enhance employee communication skills, promoting effective and impactful communication at all levels.

By following these practical steps, organizations can bridge the gap and ensure that employees clearly understand how their work contributes to the organization's overall success. Recognizing the significance of individual contributions and providing autonomy and variety within a role is essential to enhancing job satisfaction.

When it comes to job design, there is more to it than just the tasks at hand. Creating a well-rounded work experience involves considering various factors. These include establishing a conducive work environment that promotes productivity and employee well-being, implementing necessary safety measures for a secure workplace, fostering effective communication practices to encourage collaboration and understanding, nurturing a culture of teamwork that promotes mutual support and synergy, and cultivating a company culture that aligns with the organization's values and goals. By considering all these elements, job design can enhance the overall work experience and contribute to the success of both individuals and the company.

In addition to being a vital component of job design, feedback plays a crucial role in measuring performance and clarifying roles. By providing clear and constructive feedback, individuals can effectively evaluate their progress and make necessary adjustments to focus on their critical responsibilities. This alignment with organizational objectives ensures a cohesive and efficient workflow, promoting overall success and growth.

Job analysis informs job design

Job analysis is crucial for guiding job design, particularly during an organizational redesign or transition from a startup phase. In the early stages of startups, it's common for everyone to wear multiple hats, juggling various responsibilities. However, as your business expands and matures, it becomes imperative to identify and define distinct roles and responsibilities to ensure optimal efficiency and productivity.

Moving beyond assumptions and meticulously scrutinizing the tasks is vital for a thorough job analysis. You can understand each role's specific duties, responsibilities, and requirements by conducting a comprehensive job analysis. This valuable information will support informed decision-making and facilitate the organization's efficient design of job roles, ensuring optimal alignment and productivity.

> Job analysis involves systematically understanding the tasks performed in a specific role. Thoroughly analyzing the job design helps determine the activities involved. Job design involves organizing work tasks and responsibilities to optimize productivity and performance.

To conduct an effective job analysis, we need to identify the job's objectives and comprehend the tasks required to meet those objectives. Next, we must break down the job into smaller components or subtasks to precisely understand its nature. Capturing as much detail as possible is essential for comprehensively understanding the job's requirements.

One helpful approach to analyzing job design is to conduct a task inventory. A task inventory involves cataloging a list of tasks and activities needed to complete a job. This method helps us identify a job's most critical tasks and responsibilities while highlighting areas of potential overlap or redundancy.

Another valuable tool for job analysis is a job description. Job descriptions provide a detailed outline of a specific job's tasks, responsibilities, and requirements. The information in job descriptions can help us identify the skills, knowledge, and experience required to perform the job effectively. It is unnecessary to include every small task in the job description; however, it is essential to analyze these tasks so that the job description can be brought to life by managers in discussions with employees filling those jobs.

Below is a sample job description of a Global Supply Chain Director job. Notice how it highlights the key areas necessary to be successful and provides enough detail for a job candidate or incumbent to understand how they will succeed in the role:

Global Supply Chain Director

General Purpose of the Position:

Reporting to the Chief Operating Officer, the Global Supply Chain Director will develop an integrated plan and multi-year roadmap to transform the company's supply chain capabilities. In this role, the successful incumbent will develop our overall supply chain and purchasing strategy and lead the end-to-end implementation planning for success. Leading through influence, this role will work collaboratively across functions, ensuring proper execution, measurement, and accountability for meeting our customers' needs by having the right materials in the right place, at the right time, and at the right cost.

Key Responsibilities/Accountabilities:

1. Supply Chain Leadership – Develop a multi-year roadmap to establish supply chain strategy, targets, and capabilities. Develop integrated strategies across functions, policies, and procedures to create an optimal supply chain function. Ensured the security of supply, high performance, quality, and appropriate cost structures. Establish and maintain strong working relationships between the supply chain and business partners to ensure alignment of objectives and results. Maintain and share knowledge on industry best practices/benchmarks and internal/external influences on our supply chain. Focus on high-value priority initiatives that alter our cost structure and competitive standing.

2. Operations & Strategy – Direct and collaborate with demand and supply teams to forecast demand to create supply plans that ensure the availability of materials or products. Analyze inventories to determine appropriate raw material inventory strategy. Implement new or improved supply chain processes. Design and implement supply chain processes that support business strategies and are flexible to changing market conditions, new business opportunities, or cost reduction strategies. Drive decision-making, prioritization, and issue escalation to ensure timely mitigation and resolution. Determine optimal supply chain footprint capacity and capability, location analysis, make-versus-buy, capital requirements and cost benefits, and timelines. Ensure appropriate multi-sourcing strategies for critical raw materials. Understand global supply chain flows and develop strategies to optimize efficiency.

3. Fiscal Responsibility – This role will be accountable for the organization's overall raw material sourcing and purchasing targets. The Director will work collaboratively to ensure efficiency in supply chain and purchasing programs, vendor selection, and product specifications to drive appropriate cost and quality balance and fitness. Lead optimization projects across the organization globally to achieve cost savings and cash flow improvements that deliver customer needs and enable growth. Optimize the supply base through supplier expansion and consolidation efforts, as appropriate. Lead cross-site savings projects while monitoring progress and driving implementation. Accountable for understanding high-level market dynamics and providing information to operations on budget planning and budget review processes as required. Lead overall supply chain risk reduction through team development of supply chain contingencies and proactive resolution for supply/demand imbalances and disruption. Use segmentation, supported by activity-based cost-to-serve analytics, to align supply chain offerings with customer needs to increase both margin and customer service levels

4. Reporting and analysis - Establish supply chain targets and ensure delivery against established metrics for measurement of supply chain factors such as cost, on-time delivery, and quality of products and services. Measure progress through metrics; Analyze information about supplier performance or procurement program success; Meet with key global suppliers to discuss performance metrics, provide performance feedback, or discuss production forecasts or changes.

Competencies Needed for Success

- *Strong analytical and decision-making skills*

- *Leadership and team-building skills*

- *Business acumen*

- *Strong communication and relationship-building skills*

- *Technical background and understanding*

Knowledge and Skill Preferred:

- *Bachelor's Degree in Supply Chain, Business, Engineering, or another related field*

- *7-10 years of progressive experience in Supply Chain/ Operations roles*

- *Experience working in a matrixed organizational environment with the ability to lead through influence*

- *Experience leading large-scale investments and capital projects*

- *Extensive experience and proven performance in Global Supply Chain and materials management or similar.*

- *Robust and pragmatic problem-solving approach with the ability to bring structure to vaguely defined problems.*

- *Proficient at composing and articulating supply strategy and business decision recommendations for review and discussion with senior management.*

- *Solid understanding of strategic sourcing and commodity strategy concepts. Distributor/Supplier dynamics & business models.*

- *Strong business partnering and interpersonal skills.*

- *Ability to work well in high-pressure situations and meet deadlines.*

Travel

Travel domestically and internationally as required.

To better understand how the job is completed in practice, we can enhance the information collected through a task inventory and job description by conducting interviews, focus groups, and observation sessions. These methods can offer further insights into job requirements and provide information about potential challenges and areas for improvement.

As you delve into job analysis, gaining a deeper understanding of the functions and processes is essential. Begin by conducting a thorough review of tasks, gradually shifting your focus towards accomplishing these tasks through functions or processes. However, analyzing a job goes beyond tasks alone. Considering the knowledge and skills required for optimal job performance is essential. Additionally, it is imperative to envision how the job will evolve, especially during company redesign or when a start-up establishes its organizational design.

Remember, this analysis is crucial to distinguishing between what we currently do and need to do. Overall, by conducting a comprehensive job analysis through effective job design, we can clearly understand the tasks and responsibilities involved in each role. This information supports informed decision-making, enables efficient organizational job design, and enhances productivity and performance.

Factors Affecting Job Design

A multitude of factors influence the complex job design process. These factors include organizational considerations, environmental influences, and behavioral aspects. These factors shape the workflow and determine the hand-offs between positions. Organizational factors, including task sequence and performer, are pivotal in job design. Work practices are critical as they directly impact task performance, affecting efficiency, effectiveness, and overall quality.

Organizations can optimize productivity, streamline processes, and ensure consistent outcomes by implementing appropriate work practices. Environmental factors, such as social and cultural expectations, as well as geographic location, have a significant impact on job design. These factors influence how jobs are structured, the tasks and responsibilities assigned, and the overall work environment. For instance, social and cultural expectations can shape the desired skills and qualifications for a particular job. At the same time, geographic location can determine the availability of resources and influence the nature of job roles. Considering these environmental factors is crucial in designing jobs that align with the organization's and its workforce's needs and context.

Behavioral factors, such as a business's growth or decline, are vital in shaping the job scope and placement within the hierarchy. By considering these factors, organizations can effectively define and organize jobs to align with the evolving needs of the business. By strategically designing job roles, businesses ensure support for growth opportunities and effective management of potential challenges. Considering behavioral factors enables optimizing the workforce, leading to enhanced overall performance.

When a job needs to be redesigned

Understanding the importance of job redesign is crucial for the success of both employees and businesses in organizational design. By proactively identifying the need for job redesign before it becomes detrimental, we can prevent individuals from shouldering the burden of ill-designed responsibilities. This approach helps foster a harmonious and efficient work environment, ensuring new roles are adequately crafted and aligned.

For example, imagine a company that wants to implement a new software system to streamline its operations, done entirely on paper.....by hand. Instead of simply assigning employees to use the software without proper training or job redesign, the company recognizes the need to redesign job roles and responsibilities. They involve employees in the process, gather their insights and feedback, and then create new job descriptions and workflows that align with the latest software system. This way, employees are empowered with the necessary skills and resources to effectively utilize the software and perform their roles in a new way, increasing productivity and job satisfaction.

In organizational design, being proactive and forward-thinking in job redesign is essential for fostering a thriving and adaptive workforce. By continuously evaluating and redefining job roles and responsibilities, organizations can ensure that their workforce remains agile and responsive to evolving business needs. This proactive approach allows companies to stay ahead of the curve, embrace innovation, and effectively navigate the ever-changing landscape of the modern business world.

> Redesigning a job is an ongoing process that involves analyzing the changing workplace and business environment to meet business needs. When economic changes occur, such as business growth or decline, the demands of the market change as well. Employees need to adapt to these market changes. Job design also considers the various stages of the business lifecycle and how the available talent in the market aligns with the company's needs.

During a slow talent market, it may be necessary to relax some qualifications to find suitable candidates. The removal of educational requirements for certain positions, a recent trend in job design, was particularly significant in response to the worker shortage during and after the COVID-19 pandemic. This shift allowed organizations to broaden their talent pool and consider individuals without a college degree for previously mandated advanced education roles. By doing so, organizations could tap into a more diverse and inclusive workforce, unlocking a more comprehensive range of skills and perspectives, promoting equal opportunities, and enabling organizations to adapt and thrive in a rapidly changing world.

Responsibility versus accountability

Job design is heavily influenced by two key factors—responsibility and accountability—whether for new or existing roles. Understanding the distinction between the two is crucial, as it creates a solid foundation for organizations to clearly outline which tasks are assigned to specific jobs and establish who is responsible for making decisions and ensuring desired outcomes.

Responsibility primarily focuses on task completion and can be shared among individuals. Accountability, on the other hand, emphasizes ownership of results and should not be distributed. By assigning a single person to be accountable for specific outcomes, organizations avoid the pitfall of diffuse accountability, where everyone is responsible, yet no one truly is. This approach significantly enhances role clarity and serves as a measure of job performance.

To effectively engage in job design, it's essential to consider performance expectations for individual roles. Each position requires specific skills and experiences for success.

Moreover, every job has vital result areas that directly align with organizational objectives. Ensuring the attainment of these objectives not only adds meaning to jobs but also keeps employees motivated and engaged. While some individuals may remain content in the same role for an extended period, others continuously seek opportunities for growth and development. Job design accounts for this by establishing career paths that facilitate smooth transitions between roles, allowing individuals to take on increased responsibilities and accountability as they acquire the necessary skills and experience.

By carefully considering responsibility, accountability, performance expectations, and career paths, organizations can create engaging, motivating jobs conducive to personal and organizational growth.

Where can I go?

Regarding job growth and development, having only some of the answers right away is perfectly alright. Remember, there are numerous avenues you can explore to discover exciting opportunities and make meaningful progress in your career. Whether networking with professionals in your industry, attending workshops and seminars or even taking on new challenges, each step you take toward personal and professional growth brings you closer to achieving your goals.

It's not just about moving from one job to another but nurturing skills and building expertise, which is vital in today's dynamic workforce. The emerging generations are highly motivated to progress rapidly, and various factors contribute to this drive. Firstly, the rapid advancement of technology has created a highly competitive environment where staying ahead is crucial for success. Secondly, the globalized nature of business has opened up new opportunities and challenges, constantly pushing individuals to strive for growth. Lastly, the younger generation has witnessed the fast-paced achievements of their predecessors and aspires to make their mark in the professional world.

In today's dynamic work environment, marked by a relentless pursuit of progress, the drive for rapid advancement has emerged as a defining characteristic. To effectively counter the prevalent job-hopping trend, employers must provide fulfilling growth experiences and create opportunities that continually challenge professionals in their current roles. By fostering an environment that nurtures personal and professional development, organizations can build a workforce that thrives on continuous learning and growth, ultimately leading to increased productivity and employee satisfaction.

Development paths

Establishing clear role transparency within an organization is vital for fostering clarity and comprehension among employees. It encompasses delineating specific job responsibilities and clarifying the roles of other individuals within the organization. Employees gain valuable insight into their potential career trajectories by cultivating such transparency.

To support this, organizations can implement leadership plans and competencies to guide employees in growing and advancing, creating a clear roadmap for personal development and providing employees with opportunities to progress in their careers within the same organization.

However, one challenge managers face is communicating development opportunities to employees without necessarily moving them out of their current positions if they are unprepared to take on new roles. Ensuring individuals receive appropriate support and guidance in their career growth requires careful communication and planning.

When employees express interest in pursuing a new role, it is crucial to assess their readiness. Several factors can impact their success, such as limited experience, inefficiency in current job tasks, or needing more skills for the desired position. For example, suppose an employee wants to transition from a software developer to a project manager. In that case, they may need to demonstrate their ability to effectively lead a team, manage budgets, and coordinate project timelines. Similarly, someone aiming for a sales management role should possess strong negotiation skills, a proven track record of meeting targets, and the ability to motivate and mentor a sales team.

By meticulously evaluating these critical factors, organizations can make well-informed decisions about promoting employees or offering the requisite support and training to bridge skill gaps. This comprehensive approach ensures that employees are thoroughly prepared for their desired roles, enabling them to contribute significantly and effectively to the organization's overall success. With this approach, organizations can cultivate a highly skilled and motivated workforce poised to excel in their respective areas of expertise and drive their growth and accomplishments.

In addition, it may be advantageous for individuals to remain in their current positions while the company focuses on developing potential candidates to fill future roles. Succession planning plays a vital role in this regard. Effectively communicating opportunities for skill enhancement and experience within their current roles requires skillful management. The intention is not to discourage individuals but to help them recognize alternative avenues for growth and engagement.

For instance, let's consider a scenario where an employee expresses interest in moving to a higher position within the organization. Instead of immediately promoting the individual without the necessary skills and experience, a diplomatic approach would offer them opportunities to participate in cross-functional projects or attend relevant training programs. By doing so, the employee can gradually gain the required skills and experience, ensuring a smooth transition into the new role and minimizing any potential negative impact on the individual and the company in the long run.

Transparency and engagement

Answering three simple questions can lay a strong foundation for employee development work and drive your organization toward its goals. Where do I fit? How can I contribute? And where can I go? Once you clearly understand job design, how it fits into the organization's overall design, and the purpose of each role, you can help answer these key employee questions.

Organizational Job Matrix

If you aim to establish a robust job design and growth foundation, one highly effective approach is implementing an organizational job matrix. This vital component of organizational design provides a visual representation of various jobs, levels, and functions within the company, enabling easy comparison and analysis across the entire organization.

For example, let's consider a large multinational corporation with multiple departments and hierarchical levels. Using an organizational job matrix, the company can clearly define each department's roles, responsibilities, and career paths. Setting clearly defined roles allows employees to understand their position within the organization (where do I fit?) and provides a transparent framework for career progression (where can I go?). Moreover, the matrix facilitates effective talent management, as it enables leaders to identify skill gaps, plan succession, and ensure equitable compensation across different roles and levels. An organizational job matrix is a powerful tool that enhances clarity and transparency within a company and helps align HR strategies with overall organizational goals.

Unlike creating a hierarchy of functions, where the emphasis is on the organization of tasks, the job matrix takes a different approach by establishing a hierarchy of jobs within a company. Doing so provides valuable insights into how your company grows employees through various roles and positions. This internal evaluation allows you to prioritize and allocate resources, recognize the importance of each job, and align the organization's goals with the skills and responsibilities of its employees. In contrast to focusing solely on external perceptions, such as job titles or rank, the job matrix ensures that each position's internal structure and value are well-defined and understood. This clarity promotes transparency, effective communication, and a more cohesive work environment.

By utilizing this powerful tool, the organizational job matrix, you can ensure consistent job descriptions and leadership competencies. Investing in your organizational framework will yield various benefits, including employee development, performance management, and recruitment efforts. With an expanded and comprehensive job matrix, you can solidify and enhance your recruiting and employee development practices, making them more efficient and effective. Why would you want to dodge this chance to optimize your workforce management?

Job matrix

Let's look at how a manufacturing organization is structured. In a company, various departments like manufacturing, marketing, sales, IT, and HR perform crucial functions. These functions are categorized into specific leadership bands, ensuring efficient management and coordination.

The first band in the organizational hierarchy consists of individual contributors who hold positions such as skilled clerical staff and technicians. Moving up the ladder, the next band includes supervisors and functional specialists who oversee the work of the individual contributors. Beyond that, we have mid-level managers and available experts who provide guidance and support to the lower bands. Finally, the highest band comprises senior leaders, or directors, responsible for making strategic decisions and leading the organization towards success.

The organization thoughtfully assigns each function to a specific band, categorizing jobs based on their unique requirements, responsibilities, and skill sets. This systematic approach facilitates an effective comparison of roles within functions and across different levels of the organization, providing a comprehensive understanding and enabling more accurate evaluation and decision-making processes.

Below is a sample job matrix for a manufacturing organization

Bands	Manufacturing	Marketing & Sales	IS/ IT	HR
Senior Leaders (Directors)	Director of Manufacturing			Director of HR
Mid-Level Leaders (Managers) Functional Experts	Plant Manager			Recruiting Manager HR Manager
Frontline Leaders (Supervisors) Functional Specialists	Production Supervisor Warehouse Supervisor			Benefits Specialist Recruiter
Independent Contributors Skilled Clerical & Technicians	Welder Painter Assembler Maintenance Technician			Payroll Clerk HR Assistant

Considering the equivalence of jobs can significantly aid in understanding what to expect from various organizational roles. Recognizing the importance of not assuming identical capabilities and responsibilities for different job positions is vital. For example, managers and receptionists have distinct organizational roles and responsibilities. This recognition is essential for effective management and fair assessment in any work environment because it ensures that employees are acknowledged and evaluated just and unbiasedly. By recognizing their contributions and providing an honest assessment, organizations can foster a positive work culture, boost employee morale, and encourage productivity and growth.

In practice, we can enhance the alignment of individuals with suitable roles by establishing a transparent hierarchy and comprehending the distinct competencies, achievements, and impacts linked to each position. For instance, creating a clear hierarchy in a software development company and understanding the specific technical skills, project deliverables, and client satisfaction associated with each job can help optimize team performance and employee engagement. This approach allows individuals to grow professionally within their current role and set clear expectations for advancing to higher positions. Doing so promotes professional development and establishes a transparent pathway for career advancement.

Using Job Design Day by Day

A robust job design is crucial in optimizing your recruiting and selection processes. By meticulously tailoring job roles, you can increase the odds that the ideal candidates are matched with the correct positions, ultimately leading to more successful hires.

For instance, consider a customer service role in a call center. A well-designed job and quality job description outline the necessary skills, such as excellent communication and problem-solving abilities. It would also specify the expected responsibilities, such as efficiently handling customer inquiries and resolving issues. Designing the job well increases the chances of finding candidates with the right skills and suitability for the role, improving your recruiting process's effectiveness and contributing to your organization's success.

Investing the necessary time to clarify your job design thoroughly and explicitly outline the required skills and competencies significantly enhances your chances of finding the perfect candidate for the role. Having this valuable information at your disposal empowers you to effectively communicate the intricacies of the position to potential candidates, ensuring a better understanding of what is expected. Additionally, it allows you to accurately assess their ability to fulfill the role, leading to a more informed decision-making process.

For instance, let's say you are hiring for a project manager role in a software development company. Clarifying the job design would involve specifying the project management methodologies and tools required and the technical skills necessary to oversee software development projects. By clearly outlining these requirements, you can attract candidates with the right expertise that aligns with your organization's needs. Implementing this approach saves time and effort in the hiring process and increases the chances of finding a candidate who can excel in the role and contribute to the success of your projects. It also ensures a better candidate experience by providing clarity to job seekers, ensuring those who apply would be fulfilled by the role, and limiting applications of those for whom this role, as we want it performed, is just the wrong fit.

Prioritizing solid job design sets you up for recruiting and selection success. When you have a well-designed job, it's like finding the perfect puzzle piece for your team. It fits seamlessly, ensuring a smooth hiring process and a workforce that works together like a well-oiled machine. Plus, it helps avoid the classic "square peg in a round hole" situation. So, remember, good job design is the key to finding the right fit and avoiding any shape-shifting challenges along the way!

Onboarding

Proper onboarding sets the foundation for employee success by helping them understand the organization and how their roles fit right from the start. Successful onboarding requires a solid job design, as it requires communication of a variety of items to new hires: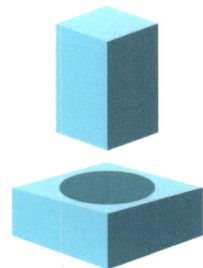

- Articulation of the critical tasks

- Ability to outline autonomy and decision-making hierarchy

- Responsibilities

- Accountabilities

- Explanation of the workflow and how the role fits with the rest of the organization

- Clearly outlined handoffs from one job to the next

- Explanation of where employees can go to find support

Managers should communicate essential tasks, such as decision-making hierarchy and employee autonomy, to ensure successful onboarding. For example, a manager could explain to a new employee that they are responsible for handling customer complaints up to a certain level, empowering them to make decisions within that scope. Clarity in job design is crucial in defining employee accountability and responsibilities. Effective onboarding also involves informing employees about their position, workflow expectations, and how their role contributes to the organization. By facilitating seamless transitions between job responsibilities, onboarding helps employees quickly and smoothly adapt to new tasks.

Providing employees with the necessary support is crucial for a successful hire. But where can they find this support? In the modern workforce, effective onboarding programs go beyond day one cultural orientation and prioritize functional aspects. For instance, providing employees access to digital tools and online training platforms can help them quickly adapt to new workflows and boost their productivity. A well-designed job onboarding program empowers employees to thrive and succeed in the digital era.

Workflow and handoffs

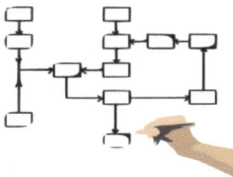

Individuals must have clear daily responsibilities to manage their work effectively. These responsibilities often involve decision-making, communication with multiple parties, collaboration with other departments or individuals, and hand-offs. A hand-off refers to transferring responsibility from one person to another and is an essential aspect of job design. In a well-established hand-off, everyone understands their role and how it contributes to the organization's objectives.

They also know the timing of the work process and who is accountable for each task.

An example of a hand-off in a workplace environment is when a project manager completes their part of a project and hands it off to the development team. The project manager ensures that all the necessary information and resources are provided to the team, clearly communicating the objectives and expectations. The development team then takes over the project's responsibility, utilizing their expertise to achieve the desired outcomes. These points of work overlap and handoffs are important components to discuss during onboarding to ensure clarity for all new employees and their co-workers and avoid frustrations that could arise.

Support mechanisms

Support mechanisms are essential in organizations as they help employees understand the hierarchy, who to approach for help, and their managers' responsibilities.

Common support mechanisms within an organization include:

- Clear hierarchy and reporting structure
- Well-defined roles and responsibilities of managers
- Accessible help resources and documentation
- Regular communication channels for seeking assistance
- Mentoring and coaching programs
- Employee assistance programs (EAPs) for personal and professional support
- Performance feedback and evaluation processes
- Training and development opportunities
- Team collaboration and problem-solving sessions
- Peer support networks and forums.

Moreover, job design is crucial in establishing expectations for employees who do not supervise others and those in managerial positions. Managers are responsible for supporting their team and ensuring employees know who to approach, when to seek assistance, and why. For example, a manager may organize regular team meetings where employees can openly discuss their challenges and receive guidance from their peers and the manager. Please refrain from sharing essential information during the onboarding process. For example, failing to provide a clear point of contact can result in a lack of role clarity. This uncertainty can leave individuals needing guidance about whom to approach for accurate and relevant information, hindering their productivity and causing unnecessary confusion.

Transforming work for greater value: a Deloitte perspective

In their insightful article, "Redefining Work for New Value,"[4] Deloitte experts challenge us to approach job redesign as more than a final objective. Instead, they urge us to see it as an ongoing process that drives creating fresh value for organizations.

Notably, the authors emphasize the importance of considering how job design impacts employees. Aligning job roles with an organization's target areas enhances employee engagement. For instance, employees can reflect on how their work influences the value the organization provides to customers, the marketplace, shareholders, and the community. This understanding promotes alignment within the organization, reinforcing the connection between job design and the company's objectives.

For example, a marketing team member may consider how their campaigns directly impact customer satisfaction and brand reputation, ultimately contributing to increased sales and market share. This awareness helps align their efforts with the organization's goals and objectives and prevents them

---

[4] Hagel, J., Schwartz, J., & Wool, M. (2019). Redefining Work for New Value: The Next Opportunity. *MIT Sloan Management Review*. https://staging.mitsmr.io/article/redefining-work-for-new-value-the-next-opportunity/

from accidentally advertising to aliens who are not yet interested in our products. After all, intergalactic sales can be quite challenging!

Trends in Job Design

Aligning job design with evolving organizational needs is crucial for several reasons. First, it ensures employees' roles and responsibilities are well-defined and aligned with the organization's strategic goals. This alignment helps to optimize productivity and efficiency, as employees understand their roles clearly and can focus on tasks that contribute to the organization's success.

Secondly, job design that adapts to changing organizational needs promotes employee engagement and satisfaction. Employees are more likely to be motivated and committed to their jobs when they feel that their organizations effectively utilize their skills and talents and assign meaningful work to them.

Lastly, effective job design can also enhance organizational agility. Organizations can quickly respond to market changes, technological advancements, and other external factors by aligning job roles with evolving needs. This flexibility allows organizations to stay competitive and adapt to new challenges and opportunities. As time goes on, both people and job requirements change. At times, what may appear to be a structural issue can be a job design problem.

We often notice this issue when a job's design differs from the organization's current goals or strategy. Common misalignment problems can impede an organization's smooth functioning and overall success.

To effectively address this problem, it is essential to carefully consider the existing role requirements and meticulously identify any new or necessary role modifications as the strategy evolves. Moreover, it is vital to consistently update and refine the job design in response to changes in goals, objectives, and organizational direction, ensuring seamless alignment with the overall strategic vision and operational framework. By doing so, organizations can proactively adapt and thrive in the ever-changing business landscape, fostering sustainable growth and success.

To ensure an organization is aligned, it is vital to consider the following questions:

- How were our jobs created? Were they intentionally designed, or did they evolve?

- Are the job roles and the connections between roles easily understandable and transparent?

- Do we have a detailed understanding of the workflow and the handoffs between different tasks to create effective job designs?

- Have we emphasized the desired outcomes, or should we focus more on individual tasks?

- Do the job designs align with the overall goals and objectives of the organization?

- If someone reads a job specification, will they be able to understand how their actions contribute to the more significant outcomes?

If the answer to these questions is no, it is crucial to establish clarity to create job designs aligned with organizational goals and objectives. Prioritize outcomes to develop concise and practical job descriptions that support organizational objectives.

> ## Are We Aligned?
>
> - Are our jobs intentionally designed?
> - Are the job design and organizational interrelationships transparent?
> - Do we understand the workflow and handoffs at a detailed enough level?
> - Have we focused on outcomes vs tasks?
> - Are the desired organizational outcomes and alignments clear in the job design?
> - What do we need to consider when we restructure work?

CHAPTER 4

The Basics of Organizational Structure

What is Organizational Structure?

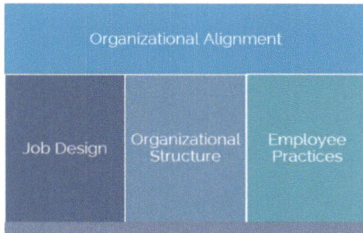

As we have discussed, an organization's structure is a critical component of the organizational design, but it's more than just a diagram of boxes and lines. The Next Step Organizational Design Framework© stands out for its unique ability to integrate structure into the overall design process. Incorporating information sharing and decision-making into how we think about organizational structure offers a genuinely innovative approach. This framework provides a comprehensive solution and enhances efficiency and effectiveness in designing and implementing organizational structures.

Organizational structure determines work and information flow and defines roles, responsibilities, and hierarchy. To be clear, the organizational structure and the job matrix talked about in the last chapter are distinct concepts. The organizational structure refers to the hierarchy and arrangement of roles within a company. The job matrix categorizes and classifies specific job functions, leveling them across and within the organizational structure.

For example, in a company's organizational structure, there may be different levels of management, such as executives, managers, and supervisors. On the other hand, the job matrix could outline various job roles like marketing specialist, sales representative, or IT technician. It is essential to recognize that although related, the organizational structure and the job matrix serve different purposes in defining the framework and responsibilities within an organization.

A well-designed organizational structure is like a blueprint that enables groups to collaborate effectively and achieve desired outcomes. It visually represents how the organization should operate, but ensuring that the structure accurately reflects its operations is crucial. For example, let's consider a tech company: The organizational structure may consist of departments such as engineering, design, marketing, and customer support. Each department has its teams and responsibilities, but they all work together towards a common goal. The structure should align with the company's goals, ensuring clear communication channels, efficient collaboration, and optimal utilization of resources. Regular evaluation and adjustments are necessary to maintain effectiveness and adapt to the organization's evolving needs.

Organizational structure includes formal reporting relationships, the number of levels in the hierarchy, and the span of control for managers and supervisors. It also considers how departments group individuals and how those departments fit into the organization. For example, this could involve creating systems that facilitate seamless communication, coordination, and integration among various departments in a workplace setting.

Information Sharing & Decision Making

At its core, organizational structure revolves around the transmission of information, the framework for decision-making, the flow of work, and the establishment of hierarchy. This framework establishes the company's knowledge flow and directives, including vertical alignment and horizontal coordination. "Vertical alignment" shows reporting and management relationships, determining the reporting relationships within an organization. This means it creates the chain of command and clarifies who reports to whom, ensuring clear lines of authority and accountability.

Meanwhile, "horizontal coordination" emphasizes information exchange among peers or colleagues in similar roles. This type of exchange encourages collaboration and teamwork. For example, employees working in different departments but at the same job level collaborating on a project would be an instance of horizontal coordination. Horizontal coordination is critical for work and information to flow across the organization.

Vertical alignment

Vertical Alignment within corporate setups refers to the seamless flow of directives and feedback from executives to operational staff and vice versa. It acts as the organizational 'rudder,' steering tasks following overarching strategic objectives. This system is critical in ensuring alignment with company goals and providing upper management clear insight into each division's accomplishments and daily workings. The structured approach harmonizes the company's trajectory across all its workflow tiers.

Vertical alignment also facilitates understanding of the rules across all levels of the organization. It allows the top management, primarily responsible for planning, to strategize effectively by comprehending the activities that originate from the lower levels. Transparency is critical to fostering a cohesive and well-informed environment.

In an organization, goals are implemented from the top down, while activities and accomplishments are reported from the bottom up. This intentional design creates a hierarchical referral system known as vertical alignment. The hierarchy within an organization works by delegating authority and responsibilities to different levels. Various organizational levels contain groups of jobs based on their roles and functions.

Here are some practical, real-world examples:

- ***Entry-level positions:*** These roles are usually the starting point for individuals entering a specific field or industry. Examples include receptionists, interns, and customer service representatives.

- ***Support staff:*** These roles provide administrative, technical, or operational support to other departments within the organization. Examples include administrative assistants, help desk personnel, and maintenance technicians.

- ***Specialist roles:*** These positions require expertise in a specific area and often provide support to other departments or teams. Examples include IT specialists, marketing analysts, and human resources consultants.

- *Middle management:* These positions supervise and coordinate employees' work, often serving as a bridge between top-level executives and frontline staff. Examples include department managers, team leaders, and project coordinators.

- *Executive-level roles:* These positions are at the top of the organizational hierarchy and are responsible for making strategic decisions and setting the company's overall direction. Examples include CEOs, CFOs, and directors.

> Remember, these examples may vary depending on the indus-try and organization structure. Just like how jokes may vary depending on the comedian and the audience, so does the ap-plicability of these examples.

Top-down communications refer to the flow of information from higher management to lower levels within the organization. This type of communication can be formal or informal, depending on the organizational structure. Larger organizations often have more rigid and formal communication structures than smaller organizations, which are more flexible. This distinction arises primarily from the larger organizations' hierarchical structures and established procedures.

The need for coordination and control across various departments and levels of management necessitates a more structured communication approach. On the other hand, smaller organizations tend to have fewer layers of management, creating a more intimate working environment. This intimacy leads to informal and flexible communication channels, which, in turn, facilitate quicker decision-making, increased adaptability, and enhanced collaboration among employees. Seamless information flow and an open dialogue culture thrive without bureaucratic hurdles, fostering the free exchange of ideas and innovation. This nurturing environment enables small organizations to respond swiftly to changes, seize opportunities, and collectively work towards shared goals.

The level of hierarchy in an organization depends on its size and structure. The hierarchical referral system tends to be narrow in small organizations, typically characterized by a limited number of employees. This means there are fewer levels within the organizational structure, allowing for a more direct chain of command and decision-making.

On the other hand, larger organizations with a more significant number of employees may have a broader hierarchical referral system. In such organizations, there are several layers of management, each responsible for overseeing a specific set of functions or departments. This broader hierarchical structure ensures the organization can effectively manage and coordinate its activities across different levels and departments while maintaining a transparent reporting and decision-making structure. The organizational structure can significantly impact the organization's overall culture and norms. Consider this when selecting the appropriate structure. We will share many examples of structure later in the chapter, showing how the choice of structure can impact vertical alignment.

Horizontal coordination

Horizontal coordination in an organization refers to workflow and information sharing, while vertical alignment ensures that frontline work aligns with the organization's top-level goals. Horizontal coordination fosters department collaboration, breaks down barriers, and facilitates effective communication.

This collaborative approach ensures that all departments contribute to achieving organizational objectives. Rather than placing sole responsibility on a single function, it recognizes the collective effort of all departments. By prioritizing strong horizontal coordination, we foster a culture of collaboration and ensure the successful completion of tasks across the entire organization. Successful horizontal coordination is critical for customer engagement and achieving the organization's business and financial goals.

Some organizations, such as multinational corporations, deliberately integrate horizontal coordination into their organizational structures. For instance, these companies often utilize some sort of matrixed organization to integrate employees across both regions and functions seamlessly.

> One effective method for promoting horizontal coordination is to establish cross-functional project teams. These teams encourage intentional collaboration among employees, creating a shared sense of purpose and fostering ongoing coordination. Task forces, for example, can form to tackle urgent and high-priority issues, ensuring the organization takes swift action. These task forces can consist of individuals from various departments, bringing diverse perspectives and expertise together. Task forces can tackle complex challenges and drive innovative solutions by pooling resources and knowledge. This collaborative approach ensures that the organization can respond effectively to evolving demands and capitalize on emerging opportunities.

Organizations may also boost horizontal coordination by implementing formal roles within their job structure, such as assigning a dedicated liaison between marketing and sales. For instance, having a marketing sales coordinator can facilitate seamless collaboration and alignment between these two departments. This intentional implementation of a component of the organizational structure can help cultivate a culture of effective collaboration and coordination, ultimately leading to improved organizational performance and success.

Various choices within the organizational structure can enhance or detract from specific organizations' vertical alignment and horizontal coordination needs. There are no right or wrong answers here; there are simply consequences for each choice made in the organizational structure.

Centralized and Decentralized Decision-Making Structures

The organizational structure also encompasses specific organizational decision-making approaches. Decision-making can be either centralized or decentralized. It is important to note that centralized and decentralized are not standalone structures but instead refer to the decision-making process within the organization.

Centralized decision-making structures concentrate decision-making authority at the top, typically at the corporate headquarters. Major decisions generally are made at this central hub and disseminated throughout the organization. On the other hand, decentralized decision-making structures distribute decision authority to lower levels of the organization. The objective is to facilitate effective communication and functional decision-making by empowering individuals with the necessary information and capabilities to make informed decisions directly impacting their respective areas of responsibility.

Achieving the right balance is crucial. When decision-making authority is delegated too low in the organizational hierarchy, individuals might need more information or expertise to make informed choices. When decentralized organizations are geographically spread out and hold responsibility for their specific functions, lower tiers within a finance department could handle financial decisions affecting their location. Conversely, decisions affecting the European, Middle East, and African regions might be decentralized only to regional levels.

Imagine a corporation as a real-life example of a centralized decision-making structure. Here, the power to make decisions rests in the hands of a central authority, often the CEO or board of directors. This influential figure takes charge of all major decisions, from setting goals and allocating resources to crafting strategic plans. It's like a symphony, where one conductor orchestrates the harmonious movements of the entire organization.

For example, let's say that a large retail company operates under a centralized decision-making model. The company's CEO holds the ultimate decision-making power and decides on key business strategies, such as expanding into new markets or launching new products. The CEO then delegates decision-making authority to department heads responsible for implementing these strategies in their respective departments. For instance, the head of marketing may be responsible for developing advertising campaigns and promotions to support the company's expansion into new markets.

A centralized decision-making model allows for clear communication and efficient organizational decision-making. It also ensures the company's overall goals and vision align with decisions. However, it can also lead to delays in decision-making if there is too much bureaucratic red tape or a lack of communication between departments.

In general, having a centralized decision-making model provides strong leadership and direction within an organization. However, for it to function effectively, effective communication and collaboration among all levels of management are crucial, ensuring everyone is on the same page and working towards common goals.

A decentralized decision-making model empowers employees at particular levels to make decisions on the spot to satisfy the customer's needs, the process, or the business. Typically, in such a model, employees have decision-making authority up to a certain point and must ensure that those decisions align with the organization's overall goals and vision.

In general, having a decentralized decision-making model provides autonomy and speed within an organization. For it to function effectively, the levels of authority must be clear, and employees need appropriate support from their managers when decisions exceed these authorities.

When choosing an organizational structure, ensure clarity on how to make decisions under that structure.

Traditional Organizational Structures

There are five primary types of traditional organizational structures: functional, divisional, geographic, matrixed, and hybrid.

- *Functional:* In a functional organizational structure, departments are divided based on business functions such as marketing, finance, and human resources.

- *Divisional:* In a divisional organizational structure, divisions are formed based on specific products or services the organization provides, such as a clothing or technology division.

- ***Geographic:*** In a geographic organizational structure, divisions or departments are organized based on different geographic locations, such as regional offices for specific countries or continents.

- ***Matrixed:*** In a matrixed organizational structure, employees are grouped based on functional and divisional aspects, allowing for expertise and project-focused work; in a true matrixed organization, employees have direct and indirect accountability to more than one part of the organization.

- ***Hybrid:*** A hybrid organizational structure combines elements from different structures to meet specific needs, such as a mix of functional and geographic divisions in a multinational corporation.

In addition, global organizations, startups, employee-focused organizations, and virtual work environments employ alterna-tive structures considered more contemporary. Notable ex-amples of these include:

- Team-based structures: where teams collaborate and work together towards a common goal.
- Network structures: where interconnected nodes or individuals facilitate information sharing and collaboration.
- Flattened structures reduce hierarchical levels and decentralize decision-making.
- Open boundary structures: In environments with fluid boundaries, organizations foster collaboration and partnerships that extend beyond conventional limits. Within open boundary structures, notable examples encompass hollow structures, modular arrangements, and virtual frameworks.
- What do we need to consider when we restructure work?

The COVID-19 pandemic has significantly increased the significance of virtual frameworks. These frameworks may remain relevant for many industries for an extended period due to their ability to enable remote collaboration, safeguard business continuity, and reduce the impacts of physical limitations. With the ability to connect and communicate with individuals across geographic boundaries, virtual structures enable organizations to adapt and thrive in an ever-changing world. As the world becomes increasingly interconnected, embracing virtual structures becomes crucial in fostering global collaboration and driving innovation.

Functional structure

A functional structure is a traditional organizational setup where individuals are grouped based on their job functions. For example, a structure may have a company president and departments like marketing, sales, finance, and human resources underneath. This type of structure ensures clear authority and efficient resource utilization. Communication is generally moderate between functions, but it is particularly good within each function.

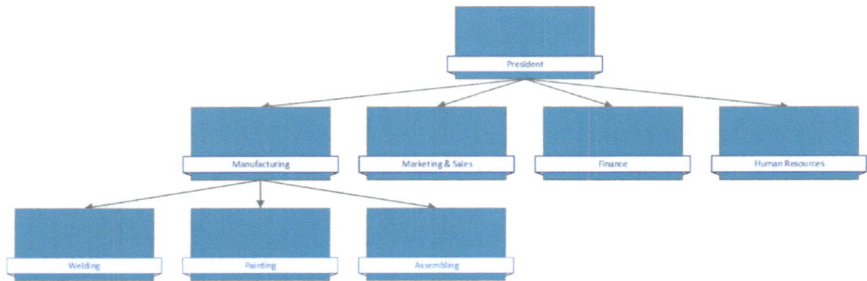

Additionally, there is typically minimal duplication of efforts among functions. Employees benefit from a clearly defined vertical professional development path; however, upward mobility between functions may be limited. As with any structure, a functional structure has challenges; decision-making can be slow, and functions may focus on their functional goals versus cross-functional objectives.

Fostering open and transparent communication channels is essential to managing these obstacles. Encouraging regular meetings, providing clear guidelines, and promoting cross-functional collaboration can help. Additionally, establishing a culture of trust and mutual respect, where different perspectives are valued, can pave the way for effective problem-solving and decision-making. By acknowledging and proactively addressing the potential obstacles, organizations can enhance coordination between groups and ensure smoother operations and better outcomes.

Geographic and divisional structures

A divisional structure is a traditional structure that organizes the company by geographic location, division, or product line. Within each division, there are often functional structures, each with its own finance, HR, and manufacturing teams. Frequently, divisions have similar organizational structures within the division to create organizational cohesion.

In many companies, the terms divisional and geographic or regional are often used interchangeably, depending on how the division is defined; however, a division does not only need to be a region but also could be a business line or a product line.

The divisional structure provides the advantages of focused resources and results. Fostering adaptability to particular business, market, or regional needs and the ease of performance tracking for particular division performance are strong positives.

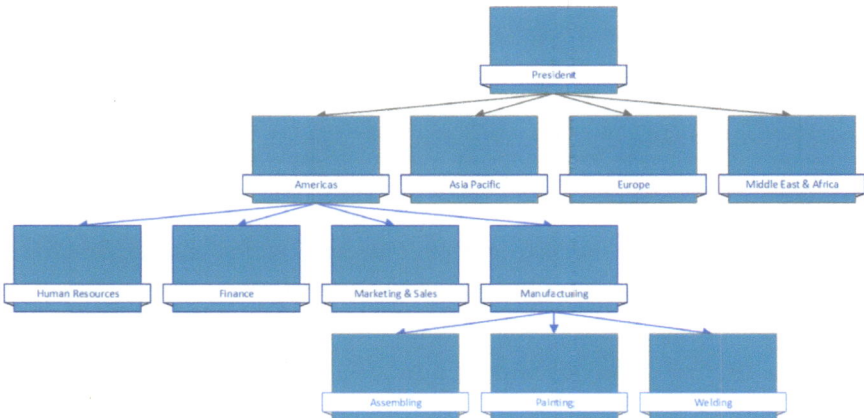

On the more challenging side, the divisional structure can result in the duplication of efforts within the company, as many things are done similarly in each division. For instance, duplicated efforts can occur when the finance team tackles a global project sub-optimized by region. Moreover, divisional competition, especially for talent, and unclear functional professional development are prevalent. For instance, navigating advancement within the finance function beyond one's division or region can take time for employees.

Matrix structure

Matrix structures are often mistaken for hybrid structures. A well-organized matrix setup resembles a grid where employees have two managers—one for the division (or region) and one for the function. For instance, if I were part of the Human Resources Department under the Widget Business, my division would be Widgets, and my direct reporting relationship would be to the head of the Widget division. My indirect reporting relationship might be with the head of the Human Resources function, thus resulting in a dual-reporting structure for my role.

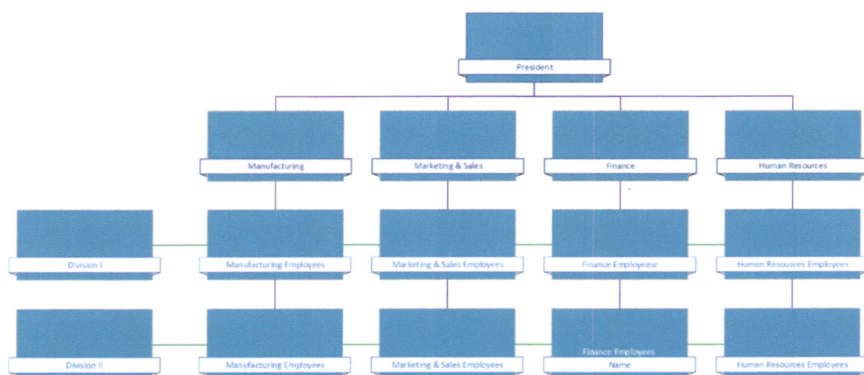

One key advantage of the matrix structure is its effectiveness in problem-solving as it integrates information from both the division and the function, aiding decision-making. It is known for its speed, flexibility, efficient resource utilization, and innovation. However, power struggles may arise, especially among employees unfamiliar with or uneasy with this setup. These conflicts between divisions and functions necessitate proficient communication and teamwork for resolution. Ensuring it is clear who has the lead for decision-making in which cases can help significantly. If not well thought out in line with the size of the business and its resources, implementing a matrix structure can incur higher costs if we add leaders for both the functions and the divisions (or regions) before we are ready.

In a matrix structure, distance leadership can take various forms, including scenarios where a manager and company leader are local, where the manager is local but the leader is distant, and even situations where both manager and leader are remote from the employees. Each setup carries unique impacts on both the company and its employees. During onboarding for such roles, it is crucial to effectively communicate the dual reporting relationships and the implications of these dynamics to employees, managers, and leaders.

Leadership versus management in a matrix organization

Every organization has a clear distinction between leadership and management. Still, this distinction becomes even more apparent in a matrix environment where employees have more than one leader, and there is the real possibility that one of them might be remote from where the employee sits. Leaders translate overarching strategies into team-specific goals and crucial deliverables. They establish precise and measurable KPIs to define the tasks for a department, division, or region. When recruiting, they delineate job specifications for the team and receive support from local managers. Leaders coach to enhance performance. The leader or manager can conduct performance-based management, which should be consistent and aligned. Effective communication and information exchange are crucial for success in a leadership role, particularly when leading remotely.

On the other hand, managers oversee operations locally, often adhering to regional regulations and guidelines, as employees follow the rules of their respective work locations. They manage personnel affairs such as absence notifications, expense claims, and timekeeping. Managers determine salaries in alignment with local policies and collect performance feedback if a remote leader is in place.

They emphasize coaching for appropriate behavior and attitudes, focusing on the "how" in accordance with local cultures and norms. Managers promote information sharing and foster belonging within the employee's local organization.

It is always good for employees to have an on-site or near manager, even if their leader or leaders are remote. Regular meetings and on-site presence by the leader and manager are crucial to fostering a thriving environment and removing feelings of isolation for employees. Establishing a local "manager" adds oversight, while cultural awareness and adherence to local laws and standards are paramount. Effective communication between the leader and manager, collaboration with team members, and a transparent relationship is critical in a matrix organization. Emphasizing feedback availability and active listening to understand diverse perspectives are vital. While different models may exist, aligning local and distant managers is essential for cohesive actions.

Newer Organizational Structures

In modern organizational setups, the spotlight shines on teamwork. It's not just about forcing teams into a formal structure; it's about blending diverse talents from various departments to tackle tasks, troubleshoot, and drive business results. Picture having a group of unassigned individuals who align with different teams as projects evolve. This approach is common in agile organizations and can shape the organizational blueprint.

Emerging trends reshape organizational norms by erasing traditional boundaries, reducing hierarchy, and emphasizing flexibility and efficiency. Within such frameworks, 360-degree feedback is prevalent, fostering direct engagement among individuals.

Team structure

During the '90s, tech firms embraced this collaborative model.

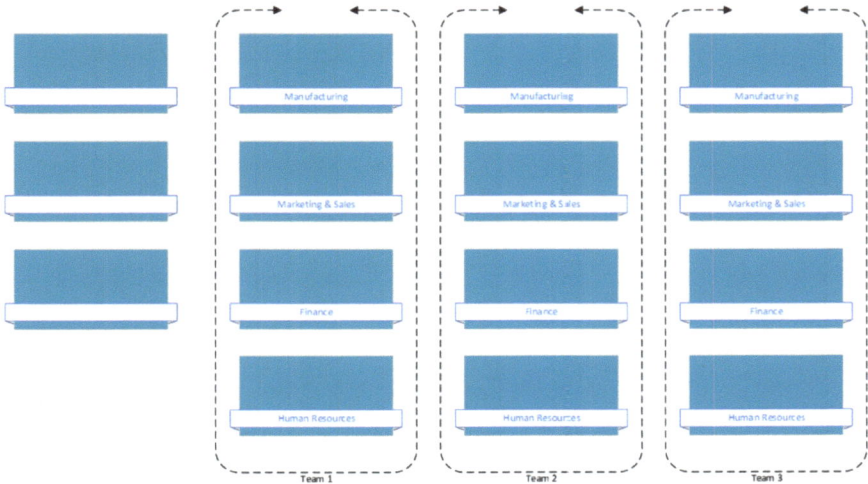

Cross-functional teams handled software platforms and collaborated with manufacturing, marketing, and finance experts. Whenever a new platform emerged, they would cherry-pick team members from the pool to form a specialized squad. With everyone's focus aligned, decisions came swiftly in this setup, fostering motivation among team members in a flat organizational structure that nurtured lateral growth.

Nevertheless, such team dynamics can stumble over time management hurdles and drown in endless meetings, hindering productivity. Success hinges on seamless team synergy; a disjointed team spells trouble. For some, ambiguity looms over career progression or even the feeling of security of ongoing employment, especially when transitioning within the department, and this needs to be clarified. For instance, navigating growth prospects within the finance team may pose a challenge if moving beyond the team boundary seems inevitable.

Network structure

Network structures are particularly effective for small businesses and organizations. Typically, a central team comprises heads of departments like

Manufacturing, Marketing, Finance, and Human Resources. This core team may utilize consultants and outsourcing for various functions, even Human Resources.

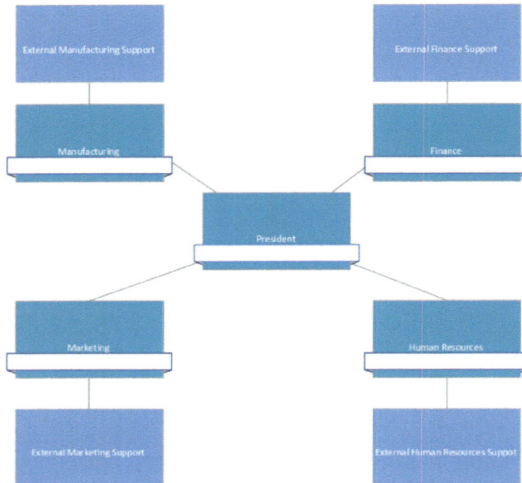

The flexibility of network structures allows for easy adaptation by including or removing consultants, keeping costs optimized. Moreover, staying up-to-date with trends is a natural outcome as outsourced vendors strive to provide cutting-edge solutions.

Reliance on outsourcing, however, may reduce company leaders' control, as external resources handle tasks independently. Given the autonomy of independent contractors, this setup can also introduce complexities and uncertainties regarding authority.

Open boundary structure

One of the newest trends is Open Boundary Structures, which can apply to concepts like hollow structures, modular structures, and virtual structures. These structures remove traditional boundaries from organizations, minimize hierarchy, and blur the lines between inside and outside the organization.

These structures can harness the talents of resources, employees, contractors, customers, and suppliers and adapt swiftly to market shifts, fostering higher engagement. Challenges can arise when solid leadership is lacking and operational processes become time-consuming or confusing as to who owns what. Embracing innovation and maintaining a flat structure can break away from traditional patterns, fostering a more creative environment, which is especially beneficial for Research and Development (R&D) initiatives.

While boundaryless communication and instant feedback are standard for newer employees, those later in their careers may need help to adapt. Overcoming the silo mentality in a boundaryless communication setting can be demanding, yet it is essential for leveraging the experience of seasoned employees.

A **hollow structure**, for example, categorizes work and employees based on core and non-core competencies, which can effectively outsource non-core functions. This model optimizes costs by focusing on core staff and outsourcing non-core tasks, which is particularly helpful in cost-competitive industries with outsourcing opportunities.

> By leveraging such structures, organizations can streamline operations, reduce overhead costs, and focus on core compe-tencies, albeit at the expense of some control over daily func-tions outsourced to external vendors.

A **modular structure**, like a building with Legos, emphasizes product lines. It keeps core components in-house and outsources non-core parts. To effectively use a modular structure, processes and products must be able to be broken into chunks. For instance, a company may handle research and development internally while contracting out the manufacturing of a widget. The company might insource procurement and sourcing based on current strengths. Each part of the product line is modularized; some are insourced, and others are outsourced based on the process and product rather than the entire function.

In industries with strong intellectual property, the blurred distinction between company employees and external partners must be considered.

In a **virtual structure**, organizations strategically form partnerships that complement each other, fostering collaboration and synergy. In a virtual structure, organizations collaborate to present a unified front, seizing opportunities and filling capability gaps. For instance, my firm recently partnered with a benefits brokerage firm to offer a comprehensive in-house solution to their customers. They specialized in benefits, and my firm specialized in HR services. By pooling our resources, we deliver all-encompassing services to clients. This collaboration optimizes customer responsiveness by erasing physical barriers, reducing overhead costs, and harnessing the best talents from each entity. However, maintaining clear communication and trust is vital to overcome challenges like employee confusion and trust issues.

Key Structural Considerations

Understanding various structural dimensions such as delegation, a span of control, and chain of command as you build your organizational structure is crucial to effectively managing work processes and for the organization's success. Additionally, understanding your company's environment—whether it leans towards organic or mechanical and its level of specialization or standardization—is essential. Considerations like safeguarding critical competencies, enhancing coordination, minimizing hierarchical delays, ensuring measurement and accountability, and fostering flexibility play a pivotal role in determining the optimal organizational structure.

Specific business areas might present challenges when deciding on the structure. Coordinating the design offers solutions for potential issues with unit-to-unit connections. Examining these links and the cross-communication among units can uncover challenges. Establishing processes and strategies for coordinating cross-communication and unit interactions is essential. In this situation, the goal is to balance core competency protection and organizational coordination by pinpointing potential design hurdles.

Another vital aspect of structuring is establishing metrics and fostering accountability. Ensuring accountability and the ability to gauge organizational performance is crucial for achieving objectives, particularly concerning organizational alignment. Your design should incorporate robust controls to support these efforts. Organizations might emphasize units with shared responsibilities that necessitate collaboration or have performance metrics that are challenging to quantify. Companies can work towards fulfilling their objectives and goals by measuring performance and holding various divisions or groups accountable for delivering results.

Flexibility is a crucial aspect of organizational structure. It empowers organizations to evolve and thrive in a dynamic marketplace. To ensure your framework meets the organization's needs, design it to fulfill current requirements while maintaining future adaptability. Consider the potential obstacles that may necessitate flexibility along the way. This iterative process involves being willing to make continuous adjustments and fine-tune your design to accommodate evolving organizational needs. While minor tweaks and modifications are part of the ongoing design journey, major transformations like transitioning from a divisional to a functional structure or from decentralized to centralized models require substantial backing and careful planning.

It's crucial to recognize the possibility and significance of functional structures nested within others to navigate the coexistence of multiple structures. Understanding the benefits and challenges unique to each structure is paramount in driving business outcomes. Understanding how these structures interact is crucial when managing a mix of structures or restructuring organizations during periods of growth and development. You can minimize drastic shifts that impede productivity and efficiency by consistently assessing and adapting your design and structure to evolving circumstances, including listening to feedback on how the organizational structure is or is not working. Embracing this adaptive approach ensures continual transformation and alignment with your organization's goals.

In many organizations, various structures intertwine. When assessing and potentially redesigning an organization, we should skillfully analyze the organization, identify its structures, and question its rationale. Subsequently, evaluate the influence on the organization's results and your employee journey.....always ask ourselves, are we aligned?

- Has our organization been intentionally designed, or has it evolved this way?
- Can we delineate our organizational structure and its rationale?
- Is it a singular structural form, or does it amalgamate various types?
- What thrives within our current structure, and what impedes our progress?
- When contemplating the most fitting structure, what aspects of our organization, business, markets, and talent should we consider?

Are we effectively harnessing our strengths and capabilities within this structure?

CHAPTER 5

Don't Forget Employee Practices

You will remember that the Next Step organizational design framework comprises three key components:

- Job design

- Organizational structure

- Employee practices

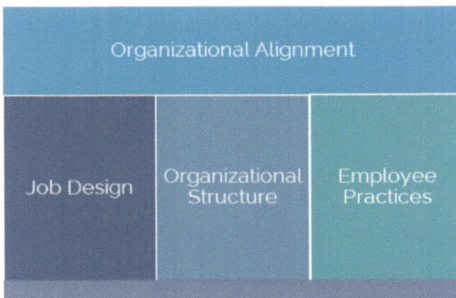

Although it may take time for many of us to become intuitive, employee practices play a pivotal role in thoughtful organizational design. Employee practices are at the heart of people operations and employee engagement, and it is critical to ensure they are thought through in the context of organizational design.

Employee practices can either bolster or impede the intentions and ultimate goals of the organizational design. By aligning employee practices with organizational objectives, the design can flourish effectively.

5 Areas of Employee Practices

Delving into employee practices reveals five essential categories:

- Organizational planning and development

- Resource management

- Employee development

- Performance management

- Total rewards

This is an exciting chapter for those of us interested in establishing or enhancing our employee practices. It contains lots of templates!

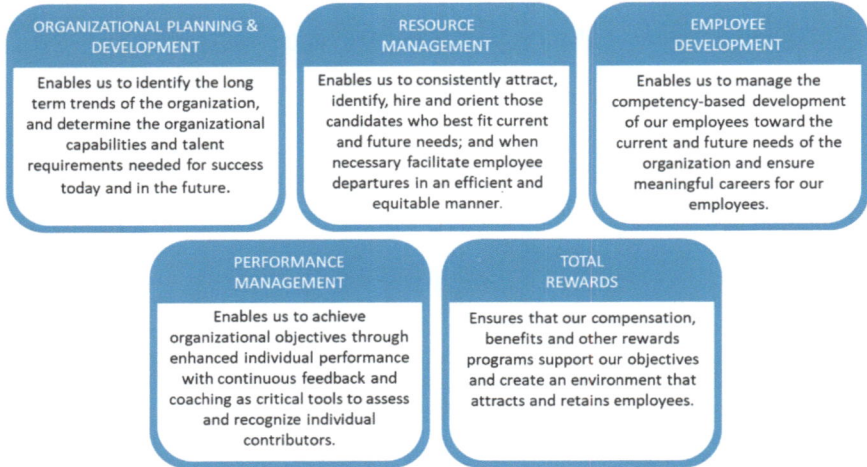

ORGANIZATIONAL PLANNING & DEVELOPMENT	RESOURCE MANAGEMENT	EMPLOYEE DEVELOPMENT
Enables us to identify the long term trends of the organization, and determine the organizational capabilities and talent requirements needed for success today and in the future.	Enables us to consistently attract, identify, hire and orient those candidates who best fit current and future needs; and when necessary facilitate employee departures in an efficient and equitable manner.	Enables us to manage the competency-based development of our employees toward the current and future needs of the organization and ensure meaningful careers for our employees.

PERFORMANCE MANAGEMENT	TOTAL REWARDS
Enables us to achieve organizational objectives through enhanced individual performance with continuous feedback and coaching as critical tools to assess and recognize individual contributors.	Ensures that our compensation, benefits and other rewards programs support our objectives and create an environment that attracts and retains employees.

Organizational Planning and Development

Organizational planning and development help us foresee the organization's long-term trends and pinpoint the capabilities and talent crucial for current and future success. This employee practice unfolds over the years, shaping the organization's path to achievement.

Some individuals stand out with high potential. Identifying them is crucial for our organizational planning. This process is sometimes called development planning or succession planning and shapes employee development. Critical alignment points exist in organizational planning and employee development practices. Understanding the current and future capabilities needed within our talent pool is vital. We must ensure we develop our talent in line with future needs. Organizational planning and development involve evaluating our company's status, identifying gaps, and strategic planning for optimal outcomes.

The image below illustrates an example of a talent assessment, sometimes called a "9-box" by your HR team. A talent assessment such as this helps pinpoint individuals within the organization who have the potential to surpass their current position.

	Need to Assess	Future and Proven Potential (Future Leaders)	
High	• Beginning to develop in their current role • New to their job, level, or the organization • Further assessment of potential is needed • Should stay in their current role for at least the coming 12-18 months to get additional development at their current job **Coach**- watch and validate; ensure competencies are being tested and assessed	• Demonstrates leadership competencies and ability to demonstrate most if not all to some degree • Ambitious- strives to expand their breadth of knowledge and experiences; aspiring to higher levels of leadership • Has potential to be promoted 1-2 levels beyond current role • Includes those ready to be promoted within the next 12-18 months and those ready to take on more global exposure **Development planning**- provide challenge learning & leadership opportunities for depth & breadth of experience; provide visibility for demonstration of competencies; give meaningful recognition & incentives; should have a formal IDP in place with clear investment by both company ($ and time) and employee (time)	
	Need to Move	Strong Professional/ Appropriately Placed	Critical Expert
	This group includes those for whom action will be required in the next 12 months; may include: • Performance improvement planning • Retirement planning • Mismatch in current position; transfer planning **Plan**- ensure a plan forward is formalized; may include formal retirement and succession/ backfill planning or documented performance improvement plan (PIP)	• Important and valued contributor at current level • Seasoned professionals or managers, well trained and experienced in their current role • May include those who do not desire move beyond current role, or we believe are appropriately placed in current role • Little change needed over the next 12-18 months. • **Performance Management**- ensure sustained performance; continue to strengthen competencies in current role through goal planning process	• Has knowledge and/ or competencies proven to be critical to HH that are difficult to replace in the market • Strong contributor in current role, but not likely to move to next level **Motivation, retention & leveraging knowledge**- provide opportunities to lead or participate in high impact projects to leverage strengths; ensure recognition of accomplishments; transfer knowledge through mentorship or training others
Low			

Career Advancement (Leadership) Potential

Low → Value of Knowledge & Competencies → High

Organizational planning and development require a deep understanding of critical roles for success and existing plans. When vital roles remain unfilled, it hampers the company's ability to achieve goals. Forecasting identifies essential roles, acknowledging not all are indispensable. For pivotal roles, contingency or succession plans should be in place to ensure operational efficiency amid expected changes. Do we have plans ready for such scenarios?

> I actually like a 5-box talent assessment better than a 9-box, because it helps those of us running the business understand clearly who goes in which box, what to do with them, and doesn't mix up a single year's performance with an individual's long term organizational potential..... one didn't really exist, so I designed one!

Engaging high-potential talent and providing growth opportunities are vital for succession planning and grooming future employees. Despite many organizations believing they excel in these aspects, the challenge lies in defining and communicating processes consistently. Flexibility is critical in organizational planning and development; readiness to adapt to evolving plans is crucial.

Just as before, we need to check that our organizational planning employee practices are aligned:

- What are the capabilities we need now, and do we have the talent in place?

- What are the capabilities we foresee needing in the future, and are we properly developing talent to meet those needs?

- What roles are critical for organizational success, and do we have plans should those roles become vacant?

- Are we ensuring that our high-potential talent is engaged in challenging work and opportunities for development?

- Do we have processes in place in each of these areas?

Resource Management

Resource management involves the processes that help us attract, identify, hire, and onboard candidates who align with current and future requirements. It also plays a vital role in managing employee departures, whether due to retirement, termination, or resignation. The employee life cycle encompasses recruiting, hiring, and onboarding, including functional onboarding and various types of orientation, as well as termination and retirement. This holistic approach ensures a smooth and equitable process throughout the employee journey.

Employee practices in resource management are vital for identifying and attracting the right talent to meet company needs. Pre-pandemic, the job market thrived with plentiful employment opportunities. However, the Covid-19 crisis triggered a talent implosion, ushering in what is now known as a significant reshuffle. As the pandemic unfolded, job losses soared, prompting individuals to seek more secure career paths or explore new opportunities. The ensuing employee burnout stemmed from staff shortages, sluggish business restarts, and resource drains, especially in hard-hit sectors like healthcare.

After the pandemic, the talent pool significantly shrank as many professionals switched fields or jobs or tapped out of traditional roles entirely. Personal adjustments, like childcare responsibilities, further reduced the workforce available for recruitment. Post-pandemic talent acquisition became complex, lengthy, and costly, leaving organizations with resource scarcity and staffing inadequacies. Having strong resource management practices remains critical to stand out in these difficult and changing situations.

To effectively manage resources and align with organizational goals, we must understand talent markets and ensure resource availability. Creating strategic recruiting points to attract talent at the right time is crucial. Developing a strong employer brand is critical to efficient recruitment. Before promoting your employer brand, crafting an employment value proposition is vital. This proposition highlights why individuals should choose your company and what sets it apart. It is integrated throughout the recruitment process to differentiate your company from competitors.

Once talent is discovered and chosen, an offer of employment is made and accepted, and employees go through onboarding.

> Effective onboarding is more than just welcoming new employees to the organization. It's about setting the stage for their success from the start.

Consider the significance of onboarding. It is said that 20%-40% of employee turnover happens within the initial 45 days and that within the first 90 days, an employee determines whether they will stay with an employer long-term. Onboarding and orientation aim to ensure that employees are introduced to the company in an enlightening manner to enhance their bond with the organization and foster commitment to its mission.

To leverage their skills early, ensure employees understand their roles and contributions. During this period it is critically important to help an employee understand where they fit and how they can contribute. A swift, thorough learning curve is critical to unlocking their potential and fostering immediate engagement. Rushed onboarding experiences risk missing out on fully integrating new hires into the company culture, leading to disengagement and a subpar onboarding journey. It's crucial to prioritize comprehensive onboarding to create a positive experience that keeps employees committed for the long term.

Below is a 30-60-90 day planning template that will allow managers and leaders to plan out what an employee's first 90 days with the company would look like. It also allows for the beginning discussions of performance management on how an employee can contribute but discussing what is expected for results in each of the key areas in the first 30, 60 and 90 days of employment.

Functional Area DEVELOPMENT	30 DAYS (Learning Phase)	60 DAYS (Develop Skills)	90 DAYS (Mastery)	Organization Resource
Enter job function here.				
Enter job function here.				
Enter job function here.				
Relationship DEVELOPMENT	30 DAYS	60 DAYS	90 DAYS	Organization Resource
Internal				
External				
Technology DEVELOPMENT	30 DAYS	60 DAYS	90 DAYS	Organization Resource
List system name here.				
List system name here.				

To check if our resource management employee practices are aligned, look at the following questions:

- Are we identifying and bringing in appropriate talent to meet our needs?

- Do we understand the talent markets well enough to ensure we will have sufficient resources?

- Are we ensuring employees are clear from the beginning on how they contribute to the company's success?

- Are we leveraging employee talent early enough in their tenure?

- Are we sufficiently ensuring that we are appropriately transitioning out when necessary?

- Do we have processes in place in each of these areas?

Employee Development

Unlike organizational planning and development, employee development centers on enhancing employees' competencies to align with the organization's present and future requirements. It's about fostering meaningful experiences and, ultimately, careers for our employees while meeting the organization's future needs. Employee development, which includes

training, planning, and leadership initiatives, answers the key employee engagement question, "Where can I go?"

Development planning can encompass both leadership and functional development, intertwining essential practices. Leadership development aims to enhance leadership through competency and skill development, coaching, and mentoring. It is crucial to align with organizational strategy for effective employee development. Remember that training for the current job is the organization's responsibility, while longer-term development is a shared responsibility between the company and the employee.

The organization is crucial in implementing development plans, with employers and employees driving the initiative. Employees primarily lead development plans, making significant contributions to their own professional growth. If an employee is not bought into their own professional development, any amount of work on the part of the organization will not move the needle. To ensure proper organizational alignment, development programs as an employee practice should be tailored to our purpose, values, and strategy, reflecting a clear vision for long-term talent development.

Understanding business needs and aligning capabilities to goals, objectives, and strategy are paramount. Employee practices, like coaching and mentoring, aid in achieving development goals beyond written plans. Incorporating coaching, mentoring, rotational programs, internships, or apprenticeships into development planning enhances businesses. Employee development is a long-term endeavor, requiring structured processes and planning for organizational alignment to propel us toward achieving business objectives.

Below is a straightforward template that could be used for development planning. Keep in mind that development planning is not training but rather the activity of continuing to develop skills and competencies that will support an employee's development into higher levels within the organization.

Employee Name:
Job Title:
Manager:
Date:

Leadership Competencies

Assess employee on each of the leadership competencies to give a perspective of where they are in development:

Leadership Competency	Development Assessment
Results oriented	
Business acumen	
Communications skills	
Curiosity	
Develops self and others	

Development Activities

Manager and employee should agree on leadership competency to focus on (1 or 2 maximum). For each, outline what the development activity or activities will be; progress updates should be documented.

Competency	
Development activity	
Progress assessment	

Competency	
Development activity	
Progress assessment	

An aside about internships

Throughout their evolution, internships serve as more than just a potential talent pipeline for companies. They offer educational hands-on experiences that classroom learning can't provide. Internships also act as a bridge to colleges and universities, fostering relationships and opening doors to various opportunities. Internships have become an essential part of the professional development process for students and young professionals. These short-term work experiences offer a unique opportunity to gain practical skills, make valuable connections, and explore potential career paths.

One of the main benefits of internships is the hands-on learning experience they provide. While traditional classroom education is crucial in building a solid foundation, internships allow individuals to apply the knowledge and theories they have learned in a real-world setting. This hands-on experience enhances their understanding and helps them develop essential skills such as problem-solving, critical thinking, and communication. Keep in mind that when developing internships, the most successful ones for both the individual and the organization are not simply free summer labor (in fact, today, most of them are paid!) but rather well-structured and planned with the goal of creating learning opportunities for students in real-world situations.

Connecting with educational institutions can help businesses explore new activities, programs, and partnerships. Even if an intern doesn't join the company permanently, they gain valuable insights to enhance their field of study and career prospects. Additionally, internships can serve as a way for companies to identify potential future employees, build relationships with top talent, and achieve short-term project-oriented results that can tangibly benefit the organization.

> ### Are We Aligned?
> - Are we training employees sufficiently to ensure they are contributing to organizational outcomes
> - Are our leadership development programs aligned with our purpose, values and strategies
> - Do we have a vision to the future on long term talent development to ensure our capabilities are sufficient to achieve our goals, objectives, and long term strategies
>   - Internships
>   - Mentoring
>   - Coaching
> - Do we have processes in place in each of these areas

Performance Management

The next category of employee awesomeness is performance management. Imagine a world where we crush organizational goals through individual superhero performances, armed with continuous feedback and coaching as our secret weapons. Forget the dusty paperwork—this dynamic process is the heart of performance management. Dive into the action with performance planning, goal setting, job juggling, feedback ninja skills, and more. It's like giving your job a makeover, ensuring everyone knows their role and rocks it!

But wait, there's more! We're talking about setting up individual objectives that sync with the big boss's goals. Personal goals are cool, but if they don't align with the organization's mission, it's like bringing a spoon to a knife fight—not much help to anyone. Let's ensure our objectives are on point and aligned with the organizational mission.

For those looking for a more templated look at a check-in, enjoy the below:

Employee name:
Job title:
Reviewer:
Check in date:

Job Performance			
General quality of work (overall standard of excellence in tasks or projects)	Exceeds ☐	Meets ☐	Needs some development ☐
Dependability (consistent and reliable performance of tasks and ability to fulfill responsibilities)	Exceeds ☐	Meets ☐	Needs some development ☐
Job knowledge (depth of understanding and proficiency an individual possesses in duties and responsibilities of their specific role)	Exceeds ☐	Meets ☐	Needs some development ☐
Communication skills (the ability to convey information effectively, express ideas clearly, and listen and comprehend messages in various settings)	Exceeds ☐	Meets ☐	Needs some development ☐
Contribution to team (actively and positively participating in group efforts and collaborating with others to achieve common goals or objectives)	Exceeds ☐	Meets ☐	Needs some development ☐
Productivity (efficiency and effectiveness with which tasks, projects or activities are completed, maximizing output and achieving goals in a timely manner)	Exceeds ☐	Meets ☐	Needs some development ☐

In what areas has the employee excelled?

In what ways could the employee make our organization even better?

As generations of employees evolve, so must our employee practices. Employees nowadays crave more than just the traditional once-a-year performance evaluations. Many organizations are ditching the old ways and embracing a more dynamic approach. They're shifting to frequent assessments, like quarterly, monthly, or even weekly check-ins. Some even toss out the formal evaluations in favor of continuous performance management. This new trend focuses on consistent coaching and feedback, meeting the expectations of today's workforce. Organizations must adapt to this change to retain the newer generation of professionals. Feedback and coaching must be ongoing to keep these individuals engaged and motivated.

Performance roundtables

Ensuring consistent employee performance evaluations throughout an organization is crucial. Within organizations, you'll encounter both lenient and strict assessors (what I call the hard graders and easy graders). Companies must establish alignment on performance assessment methods. Formal performance roundtables can play a vital role in this scenario. During a roundtable, a manager presents their evaluation, inviting challenges from colleagues, fostering alignment on performance standards, setting a benchmark.

Roundtables also allow employees to receive feedback from multiple perspectives, helping them better understand their strengths and areas for improvement. This improves the accuracy of evaluations and promotes transparency and fairness within the organization.

In addition to roundtables, organizations should have clear guidelines and criteria for evaluating performance. This helps ensure all employees are evaluated according to the same standards and criteria, avoiding potential bias or favoritism.

Managers should undergo training in performance evaluation techniques to ensure a fair and effective approach. This involves offering constructive and respectful feedback, setting realistic goals, and maintaining regular communication with employees regarding their progress.

As we close out Performance Management as an employee practice, it is important to once again check in and ensure alignment with our overall organizational design. You will notice that the final question in each of these alignment tests is.....do we have processes in place in each of these areas? These processes will be a lifesaver for you and your organization as you grow. Keep in mind that a process does not have to be rigid to be effective. Make it helpful, make it clear, and make it you!

> **Are We Aligned?**
>
> - Are our jobs clearly defined for employees so that we can outline performance expectations
> - Are individual objectives aligned with organizational objectives
> - Do employees receive appropriate feedback on performance and improvement areas
> - Are there mechanisms in place to align on employee performance across the organization when appropriate
> - Do we have processes in place in each of these areas

Total Rewards

The last category within Employee Practices is Total Rewards. In this space, we ensure that our compensation, benefits, and reward programs align with our objectives, fostering an environment that attracts and retains employees.

To be effective at utilizing total rewards as a key component of the organizational design and to support achievement of the organization's goals and objectives, we must define our compensation philosophy to establish a robust and uniform total rewards program.

Think about the following questions relative to your organization's philosophy, and remember there is no right or wrong answer, just best for you and your organization:

- Do I aim to lead in compensation?

- Do I prefer to lag in compensation?

- Do I wish to be average in the market and compensation?

- Or do I seek a balance of both worlds?

Establishing a clear compensation philosophy enables an organization to gauge suitable compensation levels and grasp employees' potential opportunities elsewhere. While striving for market competitiveness is common, it may not always be the best choice. For example, some organizations, such as a startup, may choose to lag the marketplace in base compensation but more than make up for it in equity compensation. This may focus the efforts of employees on the future success of the company.

Variable compensation plans incent and reward behaviors crucial for success. Understanding the link between behaviors, performance, and success is critical. While not the only measure of employee engagement, total rewards play a vital part in aligning their engagement with the organization to employees' and their families' needs, influencing motivation and long-term contributions.

A total rewards package is critical to employee satisfaction and retention. It includes monetary compensation and non-monetary benefits such as health insurance, retirement plans, and work-life balance initiatives. However, creating an appealing total rewards package is not just about offering attractive perks but also about promoting equity among employees.

An organization must prioritize equity to create an appealing total rewards package. Equity goes beyond legality, which differs by location globally; it embodies fair treatment among your teams. This perception of equity is essential to retaining employees. Compensation, mainly when it can be clearly explained through a compensation philosophy, reflects our organizational alignment with purpose, values, strategy, goals, and objectives.....thus showing once again how employee practices are a key component of the organizational design.

To ensure alignment of our compensation practices within the context of our organizational design, I offer again a series of self-reflective questions:

- Are our compensation levels appropriate to allow us to attract and retain the most appropriate talent to meet our organizational goals?

- Does our variable compensation plan incent and reward the behaviors and performance needed to be successful?

- Do our benefits packages provide employees with what they need to feel motivated to contribute long-term?

- Do we understand how engaged our employees are in the organization's success?

- Do we find opportunities to recognize contributions at all levels?

- Do we have processes in place in each of these areas?

The Law of Unintended Consequences

In establishing employee practices, it is important to ensure there is strong organizational alignment to purpose, values, strategy, goals & objectives. It is equally as important to guard against unintended consequences that run counter to the desired organizational outcomes. Unintended consequences are the unplanned outcomes of intended decisions or actions. These unexpected results can catch us off guard, even with a well-thought-out plan.

Example one

When implementing a quarterly sales incentive, the goal is to recognize employees' performance regularly. However, a potential issue arises if an employee falls behind in one quarter and rushes to bring in business from the next quarter to meet targets. This practice can skew quarterly figures. To prevent such unintended consequences, aligning organizational processes with purpose, values, strategy, goals, and objectives is crucial. Alignment in these areas minimizes the risk of undesired outcomes. Safeguarding against counterproductive effects is key to upholding organizational results and values.

Example two

Awards programs play a critical role in acknowledging important milestones that play a part in the success of an organization. Historically, awards for good safety performance were prevalent in manufacturing organizations. These awards have decreased in popularity due to unforeseen consequences such as failing to report safety incidents or retaliation against colleagues who experience a safety incident that has caused everyone to lose their safety bonus. This delicate balance between recognition and fostering a culture of transparency and safety awareness is a challenge many organizations face.

Are We Aligned?

I will conclude, as usual, by ensuring our alignment. An organization's design embeds employee practices. Failing to recognize employee practices as a critical component of the overall design can result in missing key areas that ultimately fail in the design's intentions.

> Do we have a clear understanding of our employee practices and how they align with the organizational strategy, goals and objectives?
>
> Do we understand how we can utilize employee practices to build needed capabilities to contribute to organizational success?
>
> Are our employee practices sufficient to attract and retain the talent needed?
>
> Have we questioned our employee practices to guard against unintended consequences?

Conclusion

Organizational design is not just about arranging boxes and lines on a chart; it is the cornerstone of enhancing organizational efficiency, effectiveness, and value creation. It involves strategically aligning an organization's structure to support its goals and objectives seamlessly. When executed effectively, it yields tangible results, fosters growth, and drives profitability, ultimately propelling the organization toward achieving its mission with a significant impact.

On the flip side, an inadequately planned design has the potential to slow down progress and obstruct the achievement of the intended goals. It can lead to a lack of clarity among team members, resulting in inefficiencies and missed opportunities. Therefore, it is crucial to delve deeper into how each organizational role interconnects and contributes to its overall success. Understanding these dynamics can provide valuable insights to pave the way for sustainable growth and long-term success.

Organizational alignment, as epitomized in the Next Step© model, serves as the bedrock of successful organizational design. This model enables individuals to grasp the organization's values, purpose, strategy, and objectives, which are pivotal for effective design. The fundamental elements of organizational design encompass:

- Job design, which involves structuring tasks and responsibilities to optimize efficiency and productivity.

- Organizational structure, which defines an organization's hierarchy, communication channels, and reporting relationships

- And employee practices that comprise policies, procedures, and guidelines that dictate how work gets done, how managers manage employees to achieve organizational goals efficiently, and how employees are rewarded and developed through their time with an organization.

> As each component unfolds, the crucial question emerges, "Are we authentically aligned?" Seamlessly navigating organi-zational alignment is achievable by thinking about the Next Step© Framework.

Effective organizational design is crucial for fostering high levels of employee engagement and achieving significant transformational results within a company. It involves structuring systems and processes that align with the company's goals and values, empowering employees to contribute meaningfully to the organization. This goes beyond surface-level initiatives like pizza Fridays or muffins in the breakroom. It requires delving deep into creating a work environment that nurtures collaboration, innovation, and continuous improvement. By establishing a robust organizational design, companies can cultivate a culture of success and sustainability, driving long-term growth and prosperity.

> Every element of organizational design must align effectively to achieve success in strategy, goals, objectives, values, and culture. This alignment ensures coherence, synergy, and a shared direction within the organization.

True organizational design establishes a deep connection between employees and the company. This alignment boosts engagement and fosters employees' sense of purpose and belonging. When considering their work, employees often reflect on three essential questions to gauge their alignment with the company's goals and values.

- Where do I fit?

- How can I contribute?

- Where can I go?

As I am sure you got from the beginning of the book, I am a huge lover of Disney and am always fascinated by its organizational design decisions. I recognize, however, that there are many other organizations that have actively embraced the ideas of organizational design and how it can drive the customer experience and, ultimately, the overall business and organizational success.

Below is a case study on the impact of organizational design written by a dear colleague of mine, Debra Parsons, of Partnership for Talent. It certainly drives home many of the points in this book and shows the true impact that thoughtful, intentional, and comprehensive organizational design can have:

Discovering the essence of organizational design and its key components that lead to success, I began applying this knowledge to my surroundings. While not as grand as Disney World, my frequent visits to a local grocery store helped me grasp how organizational design operates in everyday settings. Market Basket, a regional favorite in New England, captured my attention with its fiercely loyal customers and bustling atmosphere. The constant buzz and abundant shelves at Market Basket ensure fresh produce always awaits. This chain's strategic pricing keeps shoppers returning, showcasing a compelling tale of effective organizational design.

When I arrived at my local Market Basket, employees greeted me as they guided carts to and from the store entrance. Inside, the bustling deli department caught my eye, with staff dedicated to assisting customers. Numerous employees were busy stocking shelves in various aisles. Despite the lengthy wait in line, a consistent experience awaits me at the front of the store. The cashier's role is clear-cut—greeting each customer.

The Market Basket store's checkout process unfolds like a well-orchestrated symphony. First, the cashier meticulously scans your groceries and swiftly collects payment. As you move along, you'll notice the roles of the bagger and cashier. The bagger, stationed at one checkout, expertly packs your items. Despite its simplicity, I've witnessed the bagging process firsthand and